DEFY YOUR LIMITATIONS

TIM GAUTREAUX

Grace Lake
PUBLISHING

COPYRIGHT

CONTENTS

A WORD FROM THE AUTHOR

I don't know where you are in life right now. You might be at the pinnacle of success and happiness or you could be on the other end of the spectrum and feeling hopeless. Maybe you're struggling and your back is up against the wall financially. Perhaps money is good but, emotionally, things aren't the best. It could be that your dreams, plans, and aspirations have been hijacked by unexpected tragedy. You envy those who seem to be soaring in life. On the other hand, you could be doing better than you ever dreamed and you're ready to go to the next level.

No matter where you are, I want you to know that I've experienced both the grip of despair and the bliss of fulfillment. While our circumstances may be different, I realize the impact and effects are the same no matter who or where you are. As I reflect upon the most painful seasons and moments of my past, I now understand how powerful perspective is when it collides with raw grit. Whoever said "ignorance is bliss" was wrong. There is no reward or joy in ignorance—and certainly not in remaining ignorant, especially as it relates to personal health, growth, and development.

I unapologetically want you to know up front that I am a Christ follower. If you are not, I have no judgment for you. However, I still believe this book is for you. This is my story and my journey. My prayer for you is that you will discover and embrace what you know in your heart is right for you. I am very familiar with religious stigmas, and I'm not a fan. As a second-generation preacher's kid, my perspective and culture of self-leadership, personal growth, and individual identity were shaped by very limited and imbalanced teaching.

Growing up, healthy mentorship was lacking in my life. As a result, I was left to my own dysfunctional understanding of my life as it related to success as a leader, father, and husband. Following numerous setbacks, disappointments, and utter discouragements, I began to fight my way into health and to a better life.

My hunger for something more led me to pursue wholeness through books and other resources, and through relationships with those whom I admired. It ultimately led my heart to desperately cry out to God for strength and wisdom to be able to take hold of the life he had promised.

The result? Living my best life with my adorable wife of thirty-seven years, two amazing sons of whom I couldn't be prouder, two gorgeous daughters-in-law, a granddaughter, two grandsons, and a community of friends and mentors who are top notch. I simply want this book to be a resource to share, in hopes that you too will become the best version of yourself ... no matter where you are in your journey.

INTRODUCTION

When I was nine years old, the senior pastor at the church where my family attended in Louisiana passed away following a lengthy battle with cancer. My father had been a loyal and trustworthy protege to the pastor for quite some time. As a result, he found himself in a unique role as the appointed replacement for the senior pastor position.

Back then, churchwide votes were not common in our particular denomination. If you are currently reading this and are not familiar with the inner workings of "church life," allow me to explain. Many churches in America have procedures in place that create a democracy of sorts. By this, I mean they will allow the members to have a voice in various decisions. Some denominations will lean toward allowing a congregational voice in a broad array of decisions. Others will limit the decisions they are willing to allow a membership voice to dictate. In the case of selecting a new pastor, churchwide voting was not standard procedure.

There were pockets of unrest in the church membership. It had become apparent through certain channels of dialogue that there were mixed feelings about my father's capability to lead the church. The tension seemed to be growing by the week.

As my family drove to church this particular Sunday morning, there was little conversation, which was unusual in our household of seven. Looking back, it seems as though my parents were mentally submerged in the anticipation of the unknown.

As we walked into the church building there was a sense that everyone knew something was about to happen, but no one knew exactly what. As the choir finished leading the congregation in the last hymn, my father stepped up to take his place to preach, as was custom. However, instead of asking the congregation to open their Bible for the reading of the text, he announced that, instead of a sermon, he would lead the church in a vote. They would be given the opportunity to resolve whether or not my father would stay on as senior pastor.

The silence was quickly broken when the choir director's husband, who rarely attended our church, stood up and began to yell insults at my father. He called my father a "novice." I had no idea what a "novice" was, but by the tone he was using to communicate, I knew it couldn't have been a compliment. He also said that my father had no business pastoring any church. Another gentleman who was very loyal to my father stood up and brazenly extended an invitation to the choir director's husband to step outside to settle the matter.

My father then attempted to quiet the emotional crowd and asked the Sunday school teachers to take the children outside while the church sought resolution. I can't offer much context beyond this as to what happened inside the building, since I was one of those children. However, what I saw hours later when I re-entered the sanctuary left an indelible mark on my memory that haunts me to this day. The church was filled with people crying and yelling at one another. Judgmental fingers were pointed in outraged faces. Some left the scene as quickly as possible while others stood by trying to figure it all out.

Of everything I saw that impacted me, nothing compared to what came over me when I witnessed the emotional state of my parents. My father was absolutely broken. To this day, I've never seen such trouncing in one man's countenance. This was not my father's typical demeanor. He was always such a determined and strong man—a passionate preacher and leader who would never back down from a challenge. He was the strength of our home and family. But, this day, he was in rare form. I did not recognize the man I saw that day. Even worse, my mother was utterly devastated. It was a traumatic experience for our family.

Following what seemed like forever, we went home to pick up the pieces. Once we were all inside the house, my father left. At the moment, we didn't know why. He later returned with a U-Haul and instructed us to begin packing our things. Without much explanation, we were moving. *"Why are we moving?" "Where are we moving to?"* The response: *"You don't need to know that right now, just get to work."*

We worked tirelessly into the early hours of the following morning. Once packed and loaded, we headed to north Louisiana to what felt like the middle of nowhere. My father had family acquaintances who knew of a place where we could live if we were interested.

Our new home turned out to be a tiny log cabin deep in the middle of the hills and pines of nowhere with none of the modern amenities we had previously been accustomed to. Looking back, I realize that the secluded location provided an emotional comfort and distance from the pain that was inflicted by the individuals who had so deeply hurt our family.

This event and season of my childhood are what ultimately created the launching pad of my life.

Growing up, I was painfully shy and introverted. I could not make eye contact and was nearly paralyzed to speak during a conversation. I tried to avoid people at all costs. Because my family had chosen to live an unusually private life, I had very little interaction with society, which only contributed to my preference to isolate.

By virtue of our choice of religious beliefs, my siblings and I were taught to aesthetically stand out from the rest of the world, making our school experiences difficult. We dressed in such a way that invited ridicule from the other kids, which only compounded the desire to isolate. The further away we were from other people, the safer we felt, thinking it would eliminate the risk of being singled out.

When I was eighteen years old, I moved away from home and in with a family member in south Louisiana. My independence introduced unfamiliar opportunities to see and experience life that shocked me. The lens through which I began to see gave me the sobering sense that I was not prepared for what was ahead of me.

Everything in my life up to this point laid the groundwork for my entrance into adulthood. Just like a sponge, whatever you soak up during those formative years will inevitably be what is squeezed out of you in adulthood.

As I grew older and was faced with critical life decisions, I became more fearful. I knew I was not equipped. My perspective was unhealthy. My view of life and relationships was dysfunctional. Toxic emotions navigated me through many choices and decisions that I regret to this day. I didn't realize until much later in life that many of the decisions I would make as an eighteen-year-old would impact me as a fifty-six-year-old man. But the truth is, I didn't know what I didn't know. I didn't understand—and even to this day can't adequately convey—how much priceless possibility and potential my wrong thinking and dysfunctional view of social interaction cost me.

I had a poor view and perspective of myself. I was plagued by insecurity and thoughts that told me I was worthless and underqualified. This toxicity spilled over into all of my relationships, including the two most important ones—my relationship with God and my relationship with my wife.

The reality of raising children within the context of my messy, dysfunctional past was a scary thought. I was smart enough to know that bringing more children into an unhealthy environment would only produce more misguided adults, which would translate to more dysfunctional marriages, relationships, and children. I knew I needed to change the trajectory of my legacy but was clueless as to how to do it. And, I was utterly unaware that the solution I was searching for began with me.

On January 2, 1987, our first son was born. It would not be an exaggeration to tell you that hundreds of times throughout the course of the prior nine months, I was told that having children would dramatically change my life. Witnessing the birth of a baby is one of the most amazing encounters any human can experience. Holding my son in my arms for the first time, I immediately realized what other parents had been trying to tell me.

Becoming a father really did change my life. It changed my thinking, my view of life, and my perception of responsibility all in a split second of time. Internally, I began to ask myself, "Now what? Where do I begin?" This little guy would need round the clock attention. He would grow older and his needs would change. As his father, I wanted him to grow up to be strong, healthy, stable, and wise. This is not too much to ask for. Any good parent would want this for their child. I knew his best chances of becoming a solid adult were dependent upon the health and stability of the environment he would grow up in.

Seven years later, our second son was born. Once again, we were faced with the challenge of setting these two little guys up for success. Again and again, I would question whether or not I was equipped to raise two healthy sons. I still had unresolved issues that not only haunted my thinking, but continuously affected my closest relationships. The struggle was real. I still had so many questions. I wanted to live my best life. I wanted with all my heart to be the best version of myself for my beautiful wife and two incredible sons. That's when I began to cry out for help.

In reference once again to my childhood, I should also mention that when I was growing up, our family life was absorbed by church attendance. It was not uncommon to attend services several nights a week in addition to Sunday morning. Our church services were extremely lengthy, re-petitive, and emotionally charged. As I recall, the overtones of the entire experience were euphoric, as well as a bit con-demning, which in hindsight, only fed my insecurity.

I don't want to throw the baby out with the bath water, so to speak, as I truly believe there were sincere people with pure intentions in those churches. I also believe that the best an individual can produce is that which is formed out of the foundational resources that shaped them. I am not belittling or disregarding the purity of the intentions.

It is important to note that in our circle of churches, there was a common and overarching philosophy communicated frequently, which was that every problem in our lives must be given to God to solve. *God can fix anything.* If you were sick, God will heal you. Messed up finances? God will send more money. Broken marriage and relationships? God will put them back together.

While I believe there is profound truth to the fundamental premise that God is the answer to everything, here was the problem—there was never any real balanced teaching that emphasized the personal responsibility that belongs to us as individuals. We were taught to bring all problems to God. And if we weren't seeing results, we should just continue to "wait upon the Lord."

This culture of life was all I knew. I wholeheartedly believed this. I didn't have a reason to believe anything else. I was passionate about my faith and had no plan to change it.

As I evolved into adulthood, I became self-aware of this secretly disappointed view of God. My greatest questions revolved around "why?" Why the endless frustration? Why am I not seeing results? Why does the God I trust so much seem so distant and disconnected from my everyday life?

I felt like my faith was as strong as it could have possibly been, but, more often than not, I came up empty, discouraged, confused, and eventually angry. I did everything "by the book" but wasn't receiving what I had been promised. I gradually became depressed.

I need to pause and spend some time here because this is critical to understanding my journey of untangling the culture of a strong indoctrination that God was the literal solution for every single issue in life. Very often, my anxiety would lead me to intense quandary with regard to where God's responsibility began and ended. I would agonize over what seemed like the lack of God's involvement and what felt like the total absence of his empathy. I wondered why my marriage wasn't getting any better. I was praying and doing all my spiritual due diligence with no evidence of change on any front. Instead, I was becoming more depressed, more disposed to isolation from people, and much more disillusioned with regard to who I was or who I was supposed to become.

At the time, it didn't feel like anyone understood me. In one attempt to unpack my feelings with a trusted friend, I was told that I was just "wired wrong." It was the truth. However, there was no hopeful attempt or explanation offered as to how to rewire correctly. This only compounded the misery and confusion. As a result, I leaned in to more of an insulated approach to life. This made me feel safe and protected. I reasoned that if I could escape from the threat of being hurt by people, I would then eliminate the misery of having to deal with it.

What makes this all even more complicated is that most of my adult years have been submerged in vocational ministry. I have been involved in conceivably every church area of ministry leadership—youth, young adults, outreach, music, lead pastoring, you name it. In light of what I have described about who I was up to this point, this seems like an oxymoron. Very much like my marital relationship, I had nothing to give anyone. I was completely void of any idea as to what I had to give that would make any lasting difference in anyone's life. I ran the play. I checked boxes. I faked smiles and patronized pain and tragedy in the lives of others. I had no real clue how to authentically empathize with someone who needed hope and encouragement in times of despair. I learned all the jargon and went through the motions to make the best impression possible, but nothing I was doing came from a healthy soul. It was superficial at best, and I knew it. I knew it was wrong and broken, but I didn't know how to fix it, what to fix, or where to begin. I prayed many beautiful prayers for people without any sense of resolve that my prayer would truly make a difference. I conducted countless hours of counseling with a textbook approach, knowing that much of what I was prescribing wasn't even working for me. Some will probably read this and be shocked. However, I must be authentic and transparent here because I am convinced that I am not an exception. If honest, many in ministry can relate to my experience. It is tragic. This is one of the most vivid examples of what distinguishes religion from a relationship with Christ.

What I'm about to say may be difficult to believe, so let me make something very clear—every organization on this planet has one thing in common, and that one thing is people. And people are flawed.

There's a common perception that the inside of a church is practically perfect. Most don't have any idea what people in vocational ministry even do. I have always said that if you are looking for a perfect church and you find one, stay away because you're going to mess it up. You, like everyone else in this world, are imperfect. Therefore, a perfect human organization does not exist. However, I do believe that healthy organizations exist. There is a difference.

Throughout my years in ministry, I experienced numerous upsets, church hurts, church splits, betrayals, and deceptive political maneuvers by church leaders and other people that generated an entire list of personal reasons to justify quitting. Countless times, I've had the opportunity to rehearse in my mind what I witnessed as a nine-year-old boy when my father experienced similar circumstances.

For most of my life, my greatest fear was that I was somehow destined to bear the cross of confusion and unfulfillment. Something in me was crying for something different. I knew there had to be a better way.

There is a story about a man who, as he was passing by some elephants, suddenly stopped, confused by the fact that these massive creatures were being held by only a small rope tied to their front leg. No chains, no cages. It was obvious that the elephants could, at any time, break away from their bonds but for some reason, they did not.

He saw a trainer nearby and asked why the elephants made no attempt to get away. "Well," the trainer said, "when they are very young and much smaller, we use the same size rope to tie them and, at that age, it's enough to hold them. As they grow up, they are conditioned to believe they cannot break away. They believe the rope can still hold them, so they never try to break free."

The man was astounded. These animals could break free from their bonds at any moment, but because they were conditioned to believe that the rope is what dictates their limitations, they are bound by something that is incapable of holding them back but lack the revelation of their potential.

Like the elephants, how many of us go through life bound to a belief that we are to perform and function within the parameters of the past just because it's the way it's always been done? We are trained to think a certain way, do things a certain way, and treat people a certain way.

I realize that we are born with a unique personality and that some of how we see things and approach situations is the result of our distinctive makeup. However, I believe the most impressionable and shapeable time of our life lies within our years of childhood when we have insufficient experiences or comparisons to challenge our perspective. Unfortunately, not everyone walks into adulthood hungry to learn and eager to become the best and most effective version of themselves. In my own life, I had to reach a painful place where my hunger to learn finally outgrew my ego.

My journey to defying the limitations in my own life began with coming to a deeper understanding of how intricately we as human beings are designed. Over the next few chapters, I want to show you how this one revelation is the key to living a life of true purpose and fulfillment in every area—body, mind, and spirit.

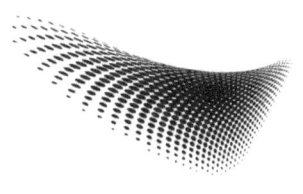

PART ONE
THE COALESCENT EFFECT

THE COALESCENT EFFECT

Scripture tells us that we are created by God and in his image. While we are limited in our knowledge about the mysterious makeup of our Creator, the Bible gives us some profound insights into the meaning of "in his image."

In John 4:24, Jesus tells the Samaritan woman that "God is Spirit." God isn't made of atoms or molecules; he isn't part of the created world. He exists in a different realm. Because he is a Spirit, God isn't limited in any way. We should not try to confine him to one place, or paint an imaginary picture of him, or restrict him to one way of doing things. We cannot put limits on God's power.

Furthermore, God is not simply a force or power—he is also a person. And, like a person, he acts, feels, thinks, sympathizes, forgives, decides, judges, and loves. There is, of course, a dramatic difference between God's personality and ours—he is perfect, but we are not. Emotions like anger, selfishness, hatred, jealousy, and pride can overtake us. But God isn't this way. He alone is perfect. Even his anger is righteous because it is directed solely against evil.

Deuteronomy 32:4 says, "…his works are perfect, and all his ways are just." God is holy, righteous, and pure. First John 1:5 tells us, "God is light; in him there is no darkness at all."

Within the context of his spiritual composition, it is important to also understand that one of the similarities in God's makeup and ours is the number three. God is triune in design—Father, Son, and Holy Spirit. Although the New Testament does not contain a fully formulated doctrine of the Trinity, it nevertheless records events and formulations that clearly depict the divine Trinity and its activity in the history of salvation.

One example of the presence of the triune God can be found at the beginning of Jesus' public ministry, when, at his baptism, the Father and the Holy Spirit attest to the sending of the incarnate Son of God:

> *Just as Jesus was coming up out of the water, he saw heaven being torn open and the Spirit descending on him like a dove. And a voice came from heaven: "You are my Son, whom I love; with you I am well pleased." (Mark 1: 10-11)*

The Son of God, as is revealed here, works in unity with the Father and the Holy Spirit.

Indicators of the bond between the persons of the Trinity can be found in John 10:30, which speaks of the oneness between the Son and the Father, and where Jesus Christ says: "I and the Father are one."

The promise of the Holy Spirit also attests to the Trinity:

> *But when he, the Spirit of truth, comes, he will guide you into all the truth. He will not speak on his own; he will speak only what he hears, and he will tell you what is yet to come. He will glorify me because it is from me that he will receive what he will make known to you. All that belongs to the Father is mine. That is why I said the Spirit will receive from me what he will make known to you." (John 16:13-15)*

There are further references to the Trinity of God in the epistles of the New Testament. They can be found in the praises of God as well as in the wording of certain blessings.

There are different kinds of gifts, but the same Spirit distributes them. There are different kinds of service, but the same Lord. There are different kinds of working, but in all of them and in everyone it is the same God at work. (1 Corinthians 12:4-6)

This previous passage refers as much to the uniqueness of God as to the different self-revelations of the divine persons.

That God's activity provides evidence of his Trinitarian nature is also attested in Ephesians 4:4-6:

There is one body and one Spirit, just as you were called to one hope when you were called; one Lord, one faith, one baptism; one God and Father of all, who is over all and through all and in all.

The salvific activity of the triune God is referenced in 1 Peter 1:2:

...according to the foreknowledge of God the Father, through the sanctifying work of the Spirit, to be obedient to Jesus Christ and sprinkled with his blood.

A clear reference to God's triune nature is found in the wording of the blessing at the end of the second epistle to the Corinthians:

May the grace of the Lord Jesus Christ, and the love of God, and the fellowship of the Holy Spirit be with you all. (2 Corinthians 13:14)

With the understanding that we are created in the image of almighty God, it is without question that the human being is complex. Humans are spirits, possess a soul, and live in a body.

There are many biblical references to validate this:

> *May your whole spirit and soul and body be kept blameless at the coming of our Lord Jesus Christ. (1 Thessalonians 5:23)*

> *For the word of God is alive and active. Sharper than any double-edged sword, it penetrates even to dividing soul and spirit, joints and marrow (body); it judges the thoughts and attitudes of the heart. (Hebrews 4:12)*

It is no wonder to me why many people never discover the insights and secrets that are linked to keys to a fulfilled life. The lack of understanding in the role each of the three components plays in our overall health and wellbeing could have a major negative impact on our goals, dreams, destiny, and quality of life. Any one of these components without the others is virtually useless as it relates to our wellbeing and productivity.

In most cases, the healthier and clearer our understanding, the better off we are. Many people spend their entire life struggling to achieve optimal wholeness, fulfillment, effectiveness, and purpose but do not have a clue how our spiritual, emotional, and physical makeup contributes to one total healthy and thriving individual.

I want to relate these three critical components to that of an automobile—the body, engine, and fuel. Without the engine, there is nothing to propel the vehicle. Without the fuel, the engine is useless (unless you are willing to push it everywhere you need to go). If I have a tank full of fuel and an engine but no body to house them, I still have nothing.

The point? What value are any of those three mentioned components without the unified connection and attachment to each other in order to perform in symphony in the movement and overall performance of the automobile? The answer is very simple—without any one of the three, you have nothing. And so it is within the context of humanity. Body, soul, and spirit rely upon each other equally in order to maximize the purpose, effectiveness, and overall productivity of the human being.

There is no conceivable way to make investments in one or two of the three and neglect the others and expect to experience a whole and abundant life. This is exactly why so many are frustrated, anxious, and aimlessly searching for significance. An individual is incomplete until and unless there are intentional, conscious, and quality and balanced investments into the body, soul, and spirit.

The Body

There are viable resources that give insight to the complexity and power of the human body. We are intricately and brilliantly composed. Our Creator designed us for maximum performance. The human body is like anything else—you will get out of it whatever you invest in it.

It's often said, "You are what you eat." Food is scientifically intended to provide the nutrition and essentials necessary to fuel the body, heal the body, and sustain us for longevity. So much of our nation's healthcare crisis is self-inflicted. Our hospitals are filled with people suffering from heart disease, high blood pressure, type 2 diabetes, and other chronic illnesses that come as a result of poor physical stewardship and eating habits.

Everything inside the human body—organs, bones, and muscles—is impacted by the blood that runs through it. So often, I hear people blame genetics for their health problems. Sadly, in some cases, it seems many are using it as an excuse to continue "business as usual" with bad habits. "This is how it was for my parents, grandparents, and great-grandparents and so I guess this is how it will be for me," is a common mindset.

Many, if not most, of the genetically inherited physical illnesses can be reversed with exercise and diet. I am not a medical doctor, but I have personally witnessed it many times. My wife is one who reversed a genetic trajectory toward type 2 diabetes with common sense daily diet habits.

In an article from NutritionFacts.org, Dr. Michael Greger states that while most deaths in the United States are preventable and related to nutrition, medical doctors receive little to no education in the world of nutrition—less than twenty hours over four years.

Another interesting article from MedicalNewsToday.com sheds light on a profound connection between our mental health and our physical condition:

> "Studies have noted that depression often appears in individuals who are overweight or obese. However, observational studies have not been able to demonstrate whether obesity causes depression, as there are many competing factors to consider.

For instance, obesity is a risk factor for a number of conditions, and so it might be that dealing with other health issues increases the likelihood of becoming depressed, rather than obesity being the cause.

Some researchers have argued that the relationship might be the other way around: depression is a risk for obesity. Others believe that depression and obesity exacerbate each other. For instance, obesity might make depression more likely to occur initially, but once depressive symptoms arise, they might compound obesity by making it harder for the individual to exercise."

Either way, there is a clear connection between the physical and emotional components. Whether or not one is more responsible than the other is beside the point. The truth is that both our emotional and physical health must be well stewarded in a manner that is beneficial to our overall well-being.

The Soul

The soul component of our being is where the mind, will, and emotions function. The human mind is complex, powerful, and mysterious. It's the central processing unit of our thoughts and our entire being. Scientifically, our mind consists of two parts—the conscious and the subconscious. The conscious and subconscious are the two modes of mental activity. The function and activity of both are important to understand in order to effectively navigate and manage health there. I'll liken the conscious portion of the mind to the camera lens on a smart phone. It operates in real time. The conscious is the now. It operates upon immediate activation. Our conscious mind leverages our five senses (sight, sound, smell, taste, and touch) for its activity. The subconscious portion would be the equivalent of the files and database inside the smart phone. Without getting too deep into the weeds, the simple reality is that the subconscious is who we really are and who we are becoming, by virtue of the things we willfully and intentionally allow our conscious mind to ingest. The conscious directs the subconscious mind. This is how we are able to turn our life around, reverse negative conditions, and create new and positive ones. Because the subconscious takes instruction from the conscious, it cannot argue the instructions.

Our thoughts are the byproducts of many things, largely influenced by our environments and, more specifically, by our human interaction in those environments. Our family, friends, bosses, and coworkers all have a significant influence on shaping how we think. The things we watch and listen to and read do as well. And, how we think translates into the lens through which we view the world. The exposure to our individual environments has everything to do with the shaping of who we are, what we ultimately become, and what we do.

Our mind is much like a creative bank. Whatever we continuously allow to enter, and whatever we consistently deposit, will determine what is produced. It becomes imperative then for the human individual to maintain awareness, charge, and discretion over the many influences of our thought life. We ultimately have control over our own thoughts, not external factors. What other people think about you (good or bad) is irrelevant unless you choose to believe it. You are the final authority on your thoughts, beliefs, and convictions. Be cautious and particular in what you allow to shape them. I choose to stay away from negative energy, negative conversations, and negative people. I love all people, but I do not have to subject myself to their culture if it is not life-giving to me. In fact, my best chance of helping them is to live a healthy life in front of them with a loving discretion in the amount of time spent with them.

A negative influence can pull you down easier and faster than you can pull them up. Think about it. If I am standing on a ledge several feet higher than you are and we lock hands and both pull, you will have the leverage advantage every single time. Many people do not realize that every influence they allow in their lives is either contributing to their emotional toxicity or to their emotional wellbeing.

I am selective in my music choices, conversations, social gatherings, and television viewing. This may seem rigid, but it's necessary if you want to be committed to a quality of life uninhibited by anything that poses a threat or compromises the proficiency of the life you want to live.

There is a wise saying that goes, "You'll never soar with eagles if you constantly hang out with turkeys." Too many people are content to dwell with turkeys while demanding the quality of the life of an eagle. It doesn't work that way. You will soar with eagles when you learn what eagles eat, how they fly, what they overcome, and then pay the price for flying in their air space. The altitude in which you dwell has much to do with how you think.

Your quality of life is a choice. Your choice of thoughts, mindset, and freedom to dream. We are made for more than mediocre. We are created with phenomenal God-given resources. Our minds have capacity far beyond what most of us will ever tap into. Our bodies can achieve what our minds choose to believe. I know of hundreds of success stories of individuals who should have succumbed to unfortunate statistics but chose to defy the odds. They made a decision to change their way of thinking, and then their life and everything around them began to change. Nothing around them changed until their thoughts did. Success around you begins within you.

Think about what would happen if the average individual today were handed a million dollars. Without a total mind makeover, it would likely be a waste of money because the level of responsibility required for managing that significant amount of money wouldn't match the mindset required to do so.

Life is a test. Every challenge or setback is an opportunity for a setup. I do not believe that life happens to you—I believe it happens for you. I have seen many try to over-power, control, and manipulate their circumstances while only compounding frustration. When our minds are con-sistently conditioned to remain where God designed them to remain, we cannot lose.

When desire is consistently implemented, it becomes dis-cipline. There comes a point when the discipline becomes a delight. The effectiveness of this process is dependent upon my willingness to continually resource my mind with faith builders. My continual exposure to things that feed healthy affirmations to my mind will only contribute to and fuel my God-given assignment on this earth.

The Bible provides numerous ways we can keep our mind in a continual state of health.

> *Don't copy the behavior and customs of this world, but let God transform you into a new person by changing the way you think. Then you will learn to know God's will for you,*

which is good and pleasing and perfect. (Romans 12:2)

For God has not given us a spirit of fear and timidity, but of power, love, and self-discipline. (2 Timothy 1:7 NLT)

We demolish arguments and every pretension that sets itself up against the knowledge of God, and we take captive every thought to make it obedient to Christ. (2 Corinthians 10:5)

…whatever is true, whatever is noble, whatever is right, whatever is pure, whatever is lovely, whatever is admirable—if anything is excellent or praiseworthy—think about such things. (Philippians 4:8)

I have been challenged on numerous occasions for believing that an individual has the power to control their thoughts. Many people believe we do not. I choose to believe we do have that power, and I practice it every day. While we may not be able to control the entrance of a thought, we can definitely decide its duration. Until we take ownership of our mind, it will remain an unattended battlefield of utter frustration.

…we take captive every thought… (2 Corinthians 10:5)

This verse is absolute and declarative. We possess the power and the authority to dictate what dominates our minds.

Not only do thoughts generate feelings, but feelings generate actions. Most of the time our actions are reflections of how we feel. Our actions then produce habits, and our daily habits ultimately determine our lifestyle.

Your best life is awaiting your best thoughts. Your best life has already been designed and destined. Don't wait another day. Begin with a mind-shift. Accordingly, make adjustments in your surroundings and associations and watch your life begin to change for the better. Become the observer of your thoughts until you are able to transform them into healthy, life-giving beliefs. Practice aligning your behavior with what you believe. It will take time. Be patient. It's worth it. The positive changes you wish to see in your life begin with the changes you're willing to make in your mind.

The Spirit

If we are created in the image of God, there is no way to despiritualize humanity. We are spirits. We live in a spiritual world. So much of what we experience is only recognized as human behavior, but the human existence on planet earth is primarily spiritual. There are two dominant spiritual forces at work—good and evil. You would be hard-pressed to find a movie that didn't have an overarching theme of either prevailing good or evil. There is almost always the villain and the hero. It's the ageless battle. Yet, many people are either naïve or reject the idea of the presence and activity of good and evil in the world.

Scripture tells us that good and evil are both supernatural forces that are active in every aspect of human life.

> For we are not fighting against flesh-and-blood enemies, but against evil rulers and authorities of the unseen world, against mighty powers in this dark world, and against evil spirits in the heavenly places. (Ephesians 6:12 NLT)

Ephesians 6:10 gives us the antidote:

> Finally, be strong in the Lord and in his mighty power.

Put on the full armor of God, so that you can take your stand against the devil's schemes.

Every day, we are faced with two options: we can lean into and trust the spirit of light and good or we can succumb to the power of darkness and evil. There is no third option. To seek such is to foolishly deny the existence of the other two. The spirit of mankind will either connect with the Spirit of God or with the spirit of Satan.

As I mentioned earlier, of the three components of human makeup, the spirit is the fuel in the tank of the vehicle analogy. If there is no spirit, there is no movement.

I believe it is vitally important for every human being to be aware that Jesus came to the earth to redeem mankind from the domination of sin and evil.

> *For God so loved the world that he gave his one and only Son, that whoever believes in him shall not perish but have eternal life. For God did not send his Son into the world to condemn the world, but to save the world through him. (John 3:16-17)*

> *Now there was a Pharisee, a man named Nicodemus who was a member of the Jewish ruling council. He came to Jesus at night and said, "Rabbi, we know that you are a teacher who has come from God. For no one could perform the signs you are doing if God were not with him." Jesus replied, "Very truly I tell you, no one can see the kingdom of God unless they are born again." (John 3:1-3)*

So, in simple terms, these verses instruct us to surrender the human spirit to the Spirit of God. This is called becoming "born again." This rebirth is to a new life of light and righteousness. The most amazing miracle that can ever happen in life is that of the birth of the Spirit of God inside the human life. This is the beginning of true fulfillment. Once we are connected back to our Source, we are complete body, soul, and spirit.

The Connection

I believe the epitome of total wellbeing is when the body, soul, and spirit are all healthy. We were designed and created to be holistic beings. You can't pray fifteen times a day, but still eat garbage food and listen to trash radio the rest of the time and expect to be an overall healthy person. Again, the majority of my time as a child was spent in church doing spiritual "stuff" but with no regard or nurturing for my physical or emotional wellbeing. Sadly, this is the case with so many believers today.

To maximize the life experience that we all desire on this earth, all three components of our being must maintain a consistent symphony of health. If my mind is sharp and pure, it is because I have made the necessary time and investments to produce that result. If my body is fit and I have energy and great physical health, it is because I have made the necessary investments of diet and exercise to enjoy the results. If I am spiritually intuitive and have the awareness of my Creator in every moment, it is because I am intentionally and daily connected in surrender and communion with God.

You can read every self-help book out there, but ultimately the solution is found in this simple principle. We are the ones who have complicated this. Between marketers and our own desire to dodge the discipline required, it becomes overcomplicated, and we lose interest. And, as a result, our lives are so fragmented, we lose efficiency and effectiveness.

As we continue this journey into the layers of the significance of our human makeup, it becomes critical to understand the connection to how this impacts our performance in this world.

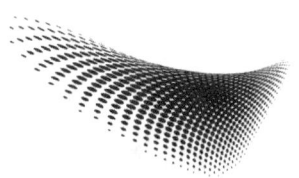

PART TWO
DEFYING THE LIMITATIONS
IN YOUR MIND

DEFYING THE LIMITATIONS IN YOUR MIND

Who Are You?

I truly believe there is something in our DNA that intrigues us to explore our identity. It doesn't take us long to figure out our distinctive differences. These manifest in a plethora of ways, from our likes and dislikes, to whether we are an introvert or an extrovert.

As kids, we would dream about what and who we wanted to be when we grew up. "I want to be a policeman," I would say. My siblings and friends would chime in with their variations of desired careers.

I have always been captivated by Jeremiah 1:5 that says, "Before I formed you in the womb I knew you, before you were born I set you apart."

This simple yet powerful sentence spoken by the Creator of the Universe emphatically implies that he knows exactly what he is doing each and every time a life is born into this world. Not only that, but there is specificity and distinctive purpose packaged within every single life. This is mind boggling when you think about it.

It never ceases to astound me when I hear statements made by people that lead me to wonder if they have any clue why they are here or what purpose their life is supposed to serve. I realize the average human is capable of articulating a conglomerate of values that are common fundamental attributes of humanity. Our lives should by default bring hope, courage, healing, and so much more to those around us. However, very few ever discover the overarching mission and distinct assignment given to them to implement during their lifetime. I was that person for most of my life, swimming in the ambiguity of what might be and what could be, but with zero definition to the "how" of getting there.

This begs the question: how in the world do we discover our purpose on this earth if we have never discovered who we are? Isn't this where we should begin this quest for purpose?

What we do is just a byproduct of who we are. What we do should never drive who we are. On the contrary, who we are should absolutely drive and define what we do. It behooves us then to quickly resolve who we are. Then, and only then, can we effectively pursue our God-given purpose.

I personally believe the greatest crisis currently on this planet is an identity crisis. I'm going to step out on a very controversial limb here. Did you know there are more than forty-six terms to describe sexual behavior, attraction, and orientation? Why does it matter, you ask? Because sexuality has everything to do with the way you identify. I believe that God, who created the universe and all mankind, is the final authority and mastermind behind the functionality of every single thing he created. He designed every one of his creations with specificity, uniqueness, originality, excellence, and precision. I am also of the opinion he never makes mistakes, so anything that attempts to function contradictory to God's design is dysfunctional.

On the other hand, I believe there is a real opponent of Creator God. His name is Satan. Satan and God have been at odds for a very long time. Satan is the twister, manipulator, liar, and perverter of truth. He enjoys confusing and deceiving people about what God has said and what he has created. Satan wants nothing more than for you to live and function outside of the parameters of God's perfect design. He knows that he will never again be back in the graces of almighty God, so he will do anything to destroy the closest thing to the heart of God—people.

The Bible chronicles numerous situations where God has to step in and correct Satan's lies. The most common of which is aimed at the identity of a person or group of people. It's a scheme that runs throughout Scripture beginning with the very first pages in the book of Genesis.

Everything God created had a source. The specificity with which God created all living things was critical with regard to identity because the role and purpose of anything always points back to its origin. If there is ambiguity and confusion in the identity, then there cannot possibly be distinctiveness in functionality or purpose.

Following the account of Creation, the Bible tells us that God gave Adam and Eve authority and dominion over the earth. He placed two trees in the center of the garden and gave them permission to eat anything from any plant they desired, with the exception of the two trees in the center of the garden.

> *Now the serpent was more crafty than any of the wild animals the Lord God had made. He said to the woman, "Did God really say, 'You must not eat from any tree in the garden'?" (Genesis 3:1)*

Scripture is clear that Eve knew exactly what God had

instructed them not to do.

> *The woman said to the serpent, "We may eat fruit from the trees in the garden, but God did say, 'You must not eat fruit from the tree that is in the middle of the garden, and you must not touch it, or you will die.'"*

> *"You will not certainly die," the serpent said to the woman. "For God knows that when you eat from it your eyes will be opened, and you will be like God, knowing good and evil."*

> *When the woman saw that the fruit of the tree was good for food and pleasing to the eye, and also desirable for gaining wisdom, she took some and ate it. She also gave some to her husband, who was with her, and he ate it. Then the eyes of both of them were opened, and they realized they were naked; so they sewed fig leaves together and made coverings for themselves.*

> *Then the man and his wife heard the sound of the Lord God as he was walking in the garden in the cool of the day, and they hid from the Lord God among the trees of the garden. But the Lord God called to the man, "Where are you?"*

> *He answered, "I heard you in the garden, and I was afraid because I was naked; so I hid." (Genesis 3:2-10)*

Don't miss this—the first sign that you have been disconnected from your true identity is that you hide in shame.

> *And he said, "Who told you that you were naked? Have you eaten from the tree that I commanded you not to eat from?" (Genesis 3:11)*

This story is tragic all the way to the end. Not only did Adam and Eve allow Satan to take everything they had, but he also stole who they were.

> *So the Lord God banished him from the Garden of Eden to work the ground from which he had been taken. After he drove the man out, he placed on the east side of the Garden of Eden cherubim and a flaming sword flashing back and forth to guard the way to the tree of life. (Genesis 3:23-24)*

Adam and Eve lost the garden and their authority, all because they believed and bought into a variation of the original master design.

Another example of God affirming the identity of one of his called is found in Jeremiah 1:5 that I referenced earlier:

> *Before I formed you in the womb I knew you, before you were born I set you apart.*

One of my personal favorites is God's affirmation of his very own Son:

> *Then Jesus came from Galilee to the Jordan to be baptized by John. But John tried to deter him, saying, "I need to be baptized by you, and do you come to me?"*

> *Jesus replied, "Let it be so now; it is proper for us to do this to fulfill all righteousness." Then John consented.*

> *As soon as Jesus was baptized, he went up out of the water. At that moment heaven was opened, and he saw the Spirit of God descending like a dove and alighting on him. And a voice from heaven said, "This is my Son, whom I love;*

with him I am well pleased." (Matthew 3:13-17)

This is incredibly powerful for two reasons:

> 1. God is *identifying* his Son to the world: *"This is my Son, whom I love."*

> 2. God is *affirming* his Son to the world: *"with him I am well pleased."*

This is critically important to note in order to fully understand what happens next:

> *Then Jesus was led by the Spirit into the wilderness to be tempted by the devil. (Matthew 4:1)*

Interestingly, this takes place immediately following baptism, identification, and affirmation.

> *After fasting forty days and forty nights, he was hungry. The tempter came to him and said, "If you are the Son of God, tell these stones to become bread." (Matthew 4:2-3)*

Please don't miss this: Jesus is hungry, weak, and alone in the wilderness. The tempter came to him and said "if." I had never noticed the power in such a small word until I read this passage again several years ago.

Let me ask you a question. Do you think Satan knew who Jesus was? Absolutely he did. I have heard teachers say that he didn't, and I strongly disagree. As a matter of fact, I don't know how Satan couldn't have known exactly who he was talking to. Otherwise, we are led to believe that Satan stumbled upon some random dude in the wilderness and was trying to guess who he was. Satan's entire objective was to get Jesus to second-guess who he was by challenging him to perform something that Satan already knew he was completely capable of making happen. What we see in these verses is Satan attacking the identity of the Son of God. As the story has it, he makes three more attempts preceded by the same powerful two-letter word "if."

There is no doubt in my mind why Satan questioned Jesus' identity in the wilderness or the significance in the timing of it. It would have never been sufficient for Jesus to only hear his Father say the words that he spoke to his Son. It was also imperative for Jesus to be given the opportunity to resolve for himself what had been spoken to him. His knowledge needed to be challenged. The challenge is what gave him an opportunity to believe or reject what had been spoken to him by his Father.

If I were to attend every karate class required to become a student but stood by as an observer never engaging in the physical training exercises, not only would I be a poor student, but I would be a failed student. In the same way, if I only say I believe something, but that belief has never been tested, it remains only a belief, not a truth. If I am proclaiming that I am a Christ follower because I attend every weekend service at my church, but my character, decisions, and actions during the week are not in alignment with the life Christ taught us to live, it makes me a liar.

So often, I see people who are filled with great information but with poor or no execution. Most people are educated beyond their level of obedience. It does neither of us any good if I affirm you and inform you with all the facts if you never take initiative to apply the information. What you believe doesn't make you a better person—your behavior does.

The information Jesus heard from his Father would have been useless had he not leaned into the value of that information with the execution of his own individual will. He had been well-resourced to confront any opposition.

As I write this, I am basking in the awe of childbirth yet again. My second grandchild was born this week. His parents named him "Fitz Timothy Gautreaux." The Latin and French meanings of "Fitz" are "son of." "Son of Timothy Gautreaux" is the actual translation of my grandson's name. This is three generations of namesake.

Most any grandparent will brag on their grandkids if given an opportunity to do so. In part, this is due to the sheer delight that comes with the continuance of the family lineage and the family name. (On a side note, I believe the other reason comes with being thankful you didn't kill your kids when you were raising them. If you are a parent reading this, let me give you some priceless advice: don't kill your kids; there are better ones coming.)

The complexity and power of the revelation associated with a new baby entering the world is quite phenomenal. Following delivery and all the formalities associated, the administrative staff of the hospital will ask the parents for a name. This is important for many reasons. The first and most significant is identity.

Identity is extremely important to understand because of the depth of its significance. Not only does my name tie me to my source, but it also ties me to the history and legacy of that source. There is a good chance that most of what you are experiencing in life today—both good and bad—can be referenced back to your parents, grandparents, and great-grandparents. I'm not talking about every detail. I'm mostly referring to how you view life, your dealings with people, the quality of your relationships, and your attitudes. We're all familiar with references like "He is just like his father" or "She is just like her mother." Not only are we genetically shaped, but we are also culturally and spiritually shaped by our preceding influencers. Our view of life is being developed from the time we're born until we leave home. At some point, our adult perspective begins to form an independence, and we may stray from pieces of various ideologies inherited from our parents and authorities, but make no mistake, the thesis of our perspective will typically point back to our family culture.

I have never met a person who wasn't in search of purpose and identity. I have met plenty who didn't know where to look or how to find it. People spend their entire lives grasping for anything they think may bring significance.

Essentially, an individual's identity has become the sum total of all that he or she can call their own. Houses, cars, clothes, jewelry, electronic devices, and our numerous possessions have become more than mere tools, luxuries, or enjoyments, but, in many cases, have become extensions of ourselves. We accumulate and leverage these things to indicate to ourselves and others who it is that we want to be and where we want to belong. And, unfortunately, we have come to believe that after we're gone, our material wealth will have marked our legacy.

Our relationship with "stuff" begins early in our childhood and throughout adolescence. It is during those formative years that our most critical comprehensions of values are shaped. The idea that we can own something, possess it as if a part of ourselves, is one that children grasp by the time they are toddlers. By the age of about six years old, they exhibit what I would call the "tightfisted effect," placing extra value on an object simply by virtue of it being or having been theirs.

As children mature into teens, we see possessions start to become a prop for the self. Anyone with experience with teenagers will agree that this appears to inevitably peak at middle adolescence, just when self-esteem has the propensity to be the lowest. And, coincidently, in addition to the obsession to own things, comes this introduction into the emotional need for flattering feedback from peers to boost their self-esteem. Through adolescence, possessions increasingly become a reflection of who a person feels they are, or at least how they would like to see themselves.

Then, in the transition from adolescence to adulthood, it may be that first car that often becomes the ultimate symbol of a person's emerging identity. I will never forget the grueling process of the first car purchase for both of my sons. It was a really big deal. And the primary reason it became such was due to the instant identity attachment that driving a particular make and model of an automobile endorses.

Once the purchase is made, teens are also very likely to make the effort to personalize their cars with stickers, unusual number plates and seat covers, as if to mark out their territory. They also tend to initially go out of their way to keep it clean in an effort to ensure the full effect. Of course, for most, this ethic eventually wanes once the newness wears off.

As our lives unfold, our possessions embody our sense of self-hood and identity still further. Material things have a way of becoming external receptacles for our memories, relationships, and travels. The house we choose to live in has much to say about our identity, as well as how much we see our things as an extension of ourselves, which also dictates in part how confident we feel about who we are. We will therefore willingly rack up enormous amounts of debt in order to set the identity bar as high as we possibly can.

Here is a recent report from Consumer Debt Statistics & Demographics in America (Debt.org):

American household debt hit a record $13.21 trillion in 2018. If you were to write that check it would read $13,210,000,000.00. Lucky for you, that debt is shared by about 300 million people.

Here's the average amount of debt for each age group:

Under 35: $67,400
35–44: $133,100
45–54: $134,600
55–64: $108,300
65–74: $66,000
75 and up: $34,500

Once again, the thing to really take note of here is the value system. Our strongest pursuits become those which are anchored to our deepest values. Our deepest values are likely entrenched in the culture we grew up in that shaped them.

The very depth (or lack thereof) of our daily disciplines, routines, and intentional activities will only rise to the level of what we value. Disciplines are only as significant as the values that bring purpose to them. My personal core values are indicators of who I am. My behavior is a byproduct of what I truly value.

I get frequent opportunities to help organizations determine the health of their culture. Throughout the process, it always becomes glaringly apparent that an organization is only as healthy as the individuals who make it up. A CEO cannot possibly expect an employee hired to work in the organization to magically begin to embrace and exhibit the organization's cultural values as they step into the threshold of the office door. They will undoubtedly bring their home culture with them and it will typically clash with the cultural value objectives of the organization's leadership. Values must be established in organizations and corporations for many of the same reasons that individuals should have them. Primarily for setting clear boundaries, decision-making, discipline, communication, customer relations, and so much more. If I don't value generosity, I will not be generous. If I don't value serving, I will not serve. If I don't value growth and health in my mind, body, and spirit, I will not value self-discipline.

Core values have so much to do with the shaping of individual identity and purpose. I do not believe you can have one without the other. I am so much more equipped to discover my purpose if I understand and have resolved who I am.

Even as a child, I was obsessed with having to know the details. My nature has always been to grind sawdust down to powder, especially where it related to a task that I was assigned to. If you are going to ask me to accomplish something, I need to have details. Therefore, I have many questions. What is the purpose? Who is it for? What is the objective? How will we know if we win? What tools and resources do I have to get the job done?

These are meaningful questions that necessitate answers and enable the individual on the mission to be effective. The more clarity I have as it relates to my assignment, the better I can resource myself with the essentials for the task at hand. Ever try to drive a nail with a screwdriver? Pretty frustrating, right? I'm so convinced that most people spend the majority of their lives not coming close to matching their design and identity with their God-given purpose. It's hit-and-miss at best.

One of the greatest tragedies in life has to be committing to something you were never called to do. What makes it more difficult is that there are so many options in today's world screaming for our attention. I remember the day when there were only a few fast-food options. (I realize how bad this ages me.) McDonald's and Burger King were the top two competing fast-food chains, so it was much easier to make a decision on where to get a burger.

The dramatically increased number of opportunities, accessibilities, and availability in our world in every arena has exacerbated our identity crisis.

From the time my boys were very young, I made it a practice to point them to the bigger picture in every situation in their lives. My oldest son went to the principal's office when he was in the third grade. He had allowed a peer to talk him into wadding up wet toilet paper and then pitching it to the ceiling until it stuck.

As soon as I became involved, I immediately took the emphasis off the fact that he had been sent to the principal's office. If I had focused solely on that issue, the message I would have been sending to my son was that he could behave however he wanted to just as long as he didn't get caught. My approach was entirely different from conventional parental discipline. Instead, I began to ask him why he would allow another person to influence him into something he knew better than to do. I followed up with, "This is not who you are." The lesson I wanted him to take away was this: never allow anyone to influence you beyond the parameters of your identity. "We don't do this," I explained to him. "This isn't who we are."

Knowing who you are immediately exposes everything contradictory to what you are to do. If I could paraphrase the scenario in the wilderness in Matthew again, it would go something like this:

Satan: "If you are the Son of God, turn those stones into bread."

Jesus: "Nope, won't do that. It's not who I am. Didn't you hear my Father?"

Who I am begins with understanding where I come from. The source determines the product. It helps to know what something is made of so there can be a healthy understanding of what can be done with it.

There are hundreds of variations of automobiles in the domestic line-up—everything from compact cars to oversized SUVs. I own a Jeep. I've had six or seven of them through the years. There are things a Jeep is designed to do that the average vehicle cannot. Mud, rocks, and inclines are no problem for a vehicle like this. It is designed to meet the challenge. I would never attempt to meet these same challenges with a Kia Soul, for example. It is not designed or manufactured for these types of terrains. It's likely we've all witnessed situations where someone made a foolish or desperate attempt to venture where their particular vehicle was never designed to take them. The result was trouble and frustration.

Many, if not most of us, will unfortunately venture into areas of life we were never designed or equipped to handle. I have marveled at times where I have observed an individual's stubborn persistence into an area that was an obvious misfit. I know people who can sing ... and I know many who cannot. It is painful to listen to someone who clearly cannot sing attempt to prove to the world they can. It breaks my heart. The reason is, they're attempting to function outside of their God-given design. I have also seen plenty of young students go through college to pursue a dream their mom, dad, or grandparent had for them. I've watched children play sports with a parent yelling on the sidelines when the child clearly wasn't made for athletics, not to mention the child's blatant lack of interest.

Ikigai (ee-key-guy) is a Japanese concept that combines the terms "iki," meaning "alive" or "life," and "gai," meaning "benefit" or "worth." When combined, these terms mean "that which gives your life worth, meaning, or purpose." Ikigai is similar to the French term "raison d'etre" or "reason for being." Very often, I've watched people get pushed away from their "reason for being" by a strong interest that overshadows their true purpose. Throughout my lifetime I have personally acquired interests and involvement in activities such as playing various musical instruments, singing, woodwork, and other hobbies. I still enjoy these activities, and you should also freely indulge in your personal interests. However, early on, if I had not been careful, some of these interests had the potential to be a distraction to my greater life purpose. We must discover our true identity, purpose, and life calling—our ikigai—not only for the personal gratification, but because this also allows us to help others in a more meaningful and significant way ... and this is the most fulfilling way to live.

If I can broaden the spectrum a bit, I would like to zoom out as it relates to what I would call the spiritual DNA every single one of us is born with. In the account of biblical Creation, there are some interesting and powerful things to note. Each time God created something, he would speak to the source of what he created. When he created the tree, he spoke to the ground. When he created the fish, he spoke to the water. The ground is the life source for the tree. If you remove the tree from the ground, it will die. Water is the life source for the fish. Everything the fish needs for life is found in the water. If you remove the fish from the water, it will die.

Something powerfully intriguing takes place when God creates mankind.

> *Then God said, "Let us make mankind in our image, in our likeness, so that they may rule over the fish in the sea and the birds in the sky, over the livestock and all the wild animals, and over all the creatures that move along the ground."*

> *So God created mankind in his own image, in the image of God he created them; male and female he created them. (Genesis 1:26-27)*

When God created the tree, he spoke to the ground. When he created the fish, he spoke to the water. But when God created mankind, he spoke to himself! Wow!

The point is that mankind was never provided a tangible life source to be connected to. Of course we must eat food and drink water to live. However, as it relates to our destiny and purpose, we were never designed to function or thrive spiritually, emotionally, or relationally through other created things. This is why money, fame, status, popularity, material possessions, or anything else that is produced by this world will never fulfill or satisfy humanity. There is only one source that fills the void of the human soul. He is the manufacturer, the designer, and the provider of every necessity required to live a meaningful and purpose-filled life on this earth. He is God. He is Creator. He is everything. He is the only one who will ever understand us because we are designed from his DNA. We are byproducts of his nature.

If God is not the designer and consultant of my life, then that leaves my destiny and purpose up to me. Human logic and intelligence are completely insufficient. They are limited at best. I may be skilled, gifted, sharp, smart, and talented, but I am completely incapable of unlocking the spiritual code of my purpose within my own resources.

1 Corinthians 2:14 sums this up well:

> *The person without the Spirit does not accept the things that come from the Spirit of God but considers them foolishness, and cannot understand them because they are discerned only through the Spirit.*

Jesus, the Son of God, came to this earth as a human. This is why it was critical for his Father to remind him who he was. He sealed his Son's identity when he spoke following his baptism. I truly believe that if that affirmation had not taken place, Jesus could have easily become the same slave so many of us have become to the things of this world. During the wilderness temptation, he was literally offered everything. Yet Satan was offering Jesus nothing that could fulfill or sustain him. Possessions and kingdoms and power were not what it would take to fulfill Jesus' mission and destiny on this earth. And if these things were insufficient for the Son of God, they will never be sufficient for you and me. Material and earthly things were never meant to be our source—they are meant to be a resource. Simply put, God is my source and earth is my resource. If we keep things in proper order and perspective, our lives are meaningful, enjoyable, and fulfilled. When we flip the roles, we get into big trouble.

It is God who knows and has pre-decided what our purpose is before we are born. Similar to attempting to take the Kia Soul through the steep and muddy terrain, he knows what and where we fit best and where we do not fit at all. There is nothing better or worse in the differences between a Jeep and a Kia Soul—they just have different designs, purpose, capacities, and capabilities. Both operate beautifully when they are performing within the parameters and guidelines of their respective manufacturer's recommendations.

It's the same with you and me. We are all uniquely different. Each one of us is powerfully effective when we are performing within the context of our God-given design.

I am not athletic. I'm five feet, six inches tall. I can't dunk a basketball. I know this. I don't even try. If I step on to a basketball court to play, I don't need anyone trying to convince me that I am a great basketball player. That's nice and all, but what I really need is for someone to tell me the truth in love: "Dude, you don't ever need to try to make a career of basketball. Period. End of story. Hang it up and pursue what you're truly wired to do."

There are so many other things that I can do—things I enjoy doing, things that produce effective results. I enjoy public speaking. I love helping people become a better version of themselves. I love mentoring. I relish one-on-one conversations that involve listening, giving perspective, and walking away with a mutual hope that things are getting better. I enjoy being a consultant where it involves troubleshooting. My analytical gift engages, and I become giddy over the fact that I know how to ask the kind of questions that will expose the obvious.

I have friends who are completely different from me—different in how they think, how they see things, and how they approach certain things. What's beautiful is that we are all okay with our differences. What would be tragic is if I were always trying to figure out how to become more like them and continuously attempting to do the things that they are gifted to do, and if they were always trying to figure out ways to become more like me and always attempting to try to accomplish things that I'm skilled and gifted to do. I'm not talking about virtues. We should all be influencers of love, hope, and kindness, for example, and should allow these virtues to inspire and change us for the better. But it's in our diversity and contentment within our God-given uniqueness and gifts that we should complement one another and the world we seek to impact.

My ultimate goal in life is to be the best version of who God created me to be. I have resolved that this will be an endeavor and journey that will take me to my dying breath. I will never be an expert on anything. It really bothers me when individuals and leaders refer to themselves as an "expert." It's a bit haughty, in my opinion. I will always be on a journey that will involve learning, tweaking, adjusting, and consistently and humbly opening myself to a better way. I am more interested in hearing about your journey and your story than I am in telling you about my own.

You may be thinking, "Well, you wrote a book so you must be very interested in telling the world your story." You are absolutely correct. However, the timeless lessons I've learned, and am still learning, have come from hundreds of hours of reading and listening to the stories of others—in books, documentaries, teachings, counseling, and other educational resources.

I have dedicated my life to two things: being a great student and being a great mentor. And most of the time, being a mentor is more about what you're doing than it is about what you're saying. Ralph Waldo Emerson once said, "What you do speaks so loudly, I can't hear what you're saying."

Defying your limitations begins with the discovery and resolve of who you are, who you were meant to be, and what you were meant to do. When you discover and resolve who you are, you have just as importantly determined who you're not. You must anchor into who you are by the standard of who God created you to be. If this doesn't happen, you'll always take your wins and losses personally, and it will rock your identity every single time.

The Poison of Comparison

Comparison is another opposing force that will attempt to diminish your identity. This has been an exhausting battle for me personally, growing up in a culture where insecurity ruled. Comparison is one of the greatest thieves of purpose and uniqueness. Individuality and distinctiveness are always in jeopardy of the bandit of comparison. Wrapped into comparison is its close friend and ally, jealousy.

At the root of both our propensity to compare ourselves and to be jealous of others is our insecurity. This comes from an unresolved discontent with who we believe ourselves to be. It is born out of the belief that we are insufficient and substandard, which compounds inferiority. None of these beliefs are fact-based until and unless we make them so. These are just thoughts we've chosen to cultivate in our minds over time on the premise of mere lies. I believe the more we feed our thoughts, the more they will grow.

Our society exacerbates insecurity through the promotion of snapshots of glamour and flashy aesthetics of the fame of Hollywood and television. Actors and celebrities portray an image that everyone desires and seems to envy. Social media is another leading contributor. We tend to try to shape our reality based on someone else's highlight reel. The majority of what we see is a farce and a facade. It is superficial and surface. This generation of youth cannot seem to capture enough selfies in order to publish an image that will hopefully return a "Like," in an attempt to appease the excruciating pain of personal insecurity and emptiness. And, in the meantime, it's as though our world is knowingly allowing a thief to rob them of their identity right before their very eyes. It's the equivalent of standing awake and alert in the middle of my own home while burglars work tirelessly and in plain sight to steal everything I own.

Comparison is a mentally debilitating losing battle. Your day gets brighter the moment you accept who you are. You are unique. You are special and set apart. You bear gifts and qualities no one else has. While there may be similarities in hair and eye color, and even voice tones, the reality is that there are no two people exactly alike. No two people think alike. No two people will ever see one thing and approach it the same way. This provides opportunity for everyone to express themselves within the context of their God-given uniqueness.

I'm thankful we're not all alike in every way. There would be no diversity to challenge the normal and ordinary. How boring would that be? One of the distinctive joys of being a father of more than one child is the reality of the difference in personalities. Two males from the same gene pool, but so distinctively different. I do not love one more than the other. I don't even love more characteristics of one more than the other. I absolutely appreciate every one of their distinctive attributes and idiosyncrasies. I love and admire them both completely.

When you begin to focus on what you have more than what you don't, you are on the road to winning. You need to learn how to celebrate yourself. I dare you to stop right now and name three things that you know people like about you. Don't tell me there's nothing. And the truth is, there are likely many things that people enjoy about you. I would encourage you to begin there. Resolve first of all that you are created by the ultimate Creator and he loves you, likes you, and has a purposeful life for you.

I understand the struggle of comparison and insecurity. I have had to fight for every bit of confidence that I have today. For a large portion of my life, every relationship I had was dominated by the thought that I was inferior. My mind was a torture chamber of enslavement to fear of what others thought about me. What was worse, I was a pathetic people pleaser. I worked hard to keep everyone happy with me because, if I didn't think I had an enemy, my happiness was intact. I was incarcerated in a mental prison I thought I would never break out of, and I still fight hard for my freedom to this day.

My utter frustration drove me to a crossroads that I believe we all must encounter at some level. It's that place where you know you have to choose a new path because the one you are currently walking will eventually lead to destruction of cataclysmic proportions. For me, it was the sobering reality that if I did not make a change in my life, my two sons would likely repeat the toxic cycle in their own. I knew that if I truly loved them, I could not allow the pain, frustration, jealousy, insecurity, doubt, fear, negativity, and misery of my past to dictate my future legacy. I wanted my sons to live fulfilled and purposeful lives. I also realized in that moment of truth that the opportunity for a better future for my family started with a better me. The decision that I was about to make would have historical and eternal impact. A change of this magnitude would require intention and resolve. As I stood between the threshold of what had been and what could be, I took the leap. My values would change, and my perspective would be different. I decided to stop allowing my feelings and emotions to dictate reality.

I did ask God for help and strength in that moment because I truly believe, as Scripture tells us, that I can do all things through Christ. However, based on the failure of the wrong teaching and the culture that had shaped my perspective up to this point, I knew this was going to require more. God was not going to descend and just zap everything into order. There was much work for me to do, much of which (and this may shock some of you) didn't require God at all. I knew I could no longer hold God responsible for things he had given me the responsibility for.

My decision to begin this journey of personal responsibility soon liberated me from the comparison trap. I realized that if I were to focus on what needed to change in my life, I had no time or energy to waste on comparing myself to others. This was my decision. It had to be.

And the same is true for you if you are willing to stand at your own crossroads and make the leap into a better life.

You'll need to resolve that God will do what he promised he would do, and you must resolve to do what only you can do. God will never force you to do anything. By the way, neither can Satan. The only power either of them has is the power we yield to them. The decisions are ours to make. I can choose the things I think about. I have the power to resolve for myself what God says about who I am. It's my responsibility, my decisions, and my freedom.

Craig Groeschel once said, "The fastest way to kill something special is to compare it to something else."

I have resolved that no one can beat me at being me. I believe that success around you begins in you—that the way you view everything around you has everything to do with the way you view yourself.

When it's all said and done, Satan doesn't need to take anything from you. He'd rather blind you from the reality that you already have it. In fact, Satan isn't after what you have at all—he is after who you are. If he can rob you of your identity, he has immediately stolen your authority and everything else that belonged to you.

Realizing who you are is not a forced intrusion by God who comes down from his throne and brainwashes you. It is a decision to believe and live out every day of your life in what you know to be true. It's a truth you need to settle in your heart once and for all. It then becomes the bedrock and uncompromised value of your emotions, so when feelings try to dictate otherwise, you can revert back to your core belief.

Comparing and people pleasing is debilitating. It will suck the life out of you. Don't confuse what I'm saying with the biblical mandate of giving honor and respect to others. Yes, we should unquestionably honor and respect people. However, we were never meant to be enslaved to the expectation of other people. It took me years to break free from this, but when I did, it felt like a 10,000-pound elephant was lifted from my chest.

If you are ever going to discover fulfillment and function within your unique and distinctive purpose, you'll need to set yourself free from opinions and comparison. How do you do this? Once your heart and mind are firmly grounded in the truth of who you are in Christ, you must daily practice a disregard for adopting what you believe everyone else thinks about you. It simply does not matter. Those who are closest to you and who have proven themselves by unconditionally investing love and trust into your life are the only ones who are qualified to supply you with authentic feedback. And even then, be true to you. Never bow and never cower to anything that is in contradiction to your God-given identity.

The Power of Affirmation

From the time my sons were barely old enough to begin to intelligibly reason, I discovered how critically important it was to affirm them. There are not many things more magical than watching the expression of a human countenance that has just received authentic, heartfelt affirmation. What makes it most impactful is when it has been given by a beloved parent, esteemed mentor, or trusted friend. Something mysteriously spiritual happens when we are reinforced by the approval and the influence of someone we truly admire and respect.

The unfortunate truth is that there is such a profound deficit of genuine affirmation today. I am not talking about flattery or empty words of manipulative fluff. There is plenty of that to go around, but it is the furthest thing from real, heartfelt, declarative affirmation. It is difficult to describe the kind of affirmation that I'm referring to with mere words, but anyone can recognize it when they receive it. It's undeniable and unmistakable. There is a craving in every human soul that can only be satisfied with the kind of nurturing that is generated from caring, sincere, loyal, and empowering words of affirmation. This can change the complexion of almost any situation. I can fall and get right back up when I have the unconditional backing and support of one who believes in me even when I don't believe in myself. My confidence is boosted beyond measure. My fear subsides. My focus is renewed, and I am motivated to defy whatever obstacle presents itself in the path of my goal.

When my boys were growing up and submerged in the world of sports, my wife and I prioritized attending every game possible. Even if both of us couldn't attend, we would make sure that at least one of us was front and center, supporting and cheering them on. Forever sketched in my memory is the expression on the faces of both of them each time they would score or execute a great play. Inevitably, following each of these scenarios, they would quickly scan the stands for the enthusiastic approval of their parents. This was typically followed by my passionate yell, "That's my boy!"

Today, my sons are adults with children of their own, and I still intentionally and lovingly affirm them. We never outgrow our need for affirmation. It will continue to be a critical necessity to our overall emotional health and productivity until we die.

Whether you're a man or woman, affirmation is critical in reaching your potential. But the reality is that many of us will never receive it from those who we desperately long to receive it from. That's something that we can't control. Even if we could, what would it have been worth if it were given out of obligation? The most valuable gifts in life are the ones that are unsolicited—the gifts given from the heart. But the answer isn't to just be tough and "get over it." There is a life transforming truth that offers hope for those of us who need to be reassured of who we are—not only is God a creator who gives purpose to his creation, he's also the ultimate Father who loves you. He is attentive to every detail of your life and knows exactly what you need. He knows you in a way that no one else does. He completely understands you. Not only does he love you, but he likes you. In fact, he is obsessed with you. He is for you and he wants more than anything for you to win. He desires for you to be blessed and to succeed. His favor goes before you. His love for you is un-conditional. God knows how many times you've messed up and still loves you. He gets your idiosyncrasies and quirks. He would run through anything to get to you and remove anything that stood between you. He created and designed you for purpose. And his voice should be louder than your noisy critics and naysayers. Knowing this is one thing, but truly believing it is another. When you resolve this truth, it's the most liberating, soul-empowering, life-giving affir-mation.

The Winning Mindset

So much of our lives is spent in passivity. We tolerate so much of what we know should be different. We become better at managing dysfunction than we are at confronting it. Why? Because we fear the unknown and so we cling to the familiar. Or, we've become so accustomed to the problem that we didn't even realize it had gotten so bad.

I remember when I went for my first eye exam. My wife had to tell me there was something wrong with my vision. I couldn't see things that she could see clearly. When I put on my glasses for the first time, I was amazed. I was blown away by what I was able to see. Being introduced to the new way of seeing was only the first step to improving my vision. That revelation also came with a newly required responsibility in order to maintain the integrity of my 20/20 vision. Contacts are uncomfortable at first. Glasses are bothersome and can be quite the inconvenience. However, I had a choice to make. I could either deal with the pain of trying to navigate half blind and risk the liability, or I could resolve that the inconvenience of the glasses and contacts were going to require a worthy consistent effort on my part.

Our resolve is refined through the challenge of pressure. It is when we are confronted with change and discomfort that we are faced with the decision to either capitulate to progress and growth, or to regression and apathy. We must rediscover the raw grit to lean into the pressures of change and challenge, for the sake of progress and for the sake of those under our influence. We must forge ahead when we see the greater good and resolve that it is a worthy battle. If it were easy, anyone could do it and everyone probably would, but what would it be worth?

If you desire to see powerful and lasting results in your life, you will need to determine what you're willing to sacrifice. Anything that costs nothing is ultimately worth what you paid for it. On the other hand, the incredible sacrifices you endured to achieve and acquire the amazing things you have are priceless. Think back to the determination you invested. The relentless spirit and passion. The refusal to quit. The tuning out of the critics and naysayers. You wanted it more than anything else and you endured the hardship because your eye was fixed on the prize.

Where is the level of your resolve today? Is it weaker or stronger than it used to be? If it is weaker, what happened? What have you compromised? What would it take to get it back? It's never too late. There's more in you! You're still breathing, your heart is still pumping blood, and your mind is still functioning. Get up and get moving. There is work to be done.

Common Culture

Cultures are byproducts of values that are shaped by beliefs. The most critical culture in the world is that of the home. A married couple must establish a shared belief system to cultivate a healthy culture in their home before adding children to the family.

I have had the honor of performing many wedding ceremonies. I have always made it a requirement for couples to counsel with me several times prior to the wedding. One of the overarching questions I always ask the couple is "What does a healthy family look like to you?"

My repeated admonition is this: whatever it is that you desire your future to be and your children to become, begin implementing the necessary changes now. Don't wait. Your growth and progress will give you the ultimate advantage of an established culture of health for your future family.

One of the tragedies of our current society is that it has become a byproduct of dysfunctional home and family culture. People don't immediately conform to a new culture because they are established products of the culture that has formed them. This is the primary cause of marital disputes.

Most arguments in marriages are primarily the result of family culture clashes. The two individuals were raised and conditioned in the different cultures of their upbringing and have very resolute but conflicting values and beliefs as a result. The beliefs engrained in the home during childhood shaped the values, and then the outcome manifests in certain behavior.

I have worked with leaders of organizations for many years and the one common challenge of every organization is creating and establishing healthy values and culture. The real kicker is that the CEO or leader of the organization is challenged with the task of dismantling the unhealthy behavior of the organization's employees while simultaneously indoctrinating the organization with healthy values, culture, and behavior. The smartest thing an employer can do these days when they are interviewing a candidate for hire is to dig deeply into the individual's personal culture. Who are they at home? What kind of husband/wife/parent/friend are they? Check out their social media posts. Take a good look at the pictures of who they're hanging with and look at the posts of those individuals as well. Seem extreme? That's the real person you'll get if you hire this individual. In my opinion, a resume is virtually useless these days. Even references can be misleading. Make no mistake, if whoever you are hiring has a distinctive image that contrasts the values and culture of your organization, they will not change just because they sit at a desk in your building.

The sad thing is that most people recognize what quality, excellence, and accomplishment look like, but few are willing to submit to what is required to achieve it.

Winners have resolved who they are, know what they believe and why they believe it, and then lead themselves every day with incessant awareness of the kind of actions required to get the results they want. For some, it meant disconnecting from unhealthy and toxic influences. They have taken authority over the now and can therefore control their future. Others have reconstructed the mental narrative of negativity.

Regardless of what you identify that is holding you back from becoming your best self, the important thing is that you make the necessary steps to adjust, and then remain consistent.

Consistency is Key

We are submerged in a society and world of fleeting fads and market-crazy initiatives—diets, workouts, fashion, and décor, just to name a few.

The problem here isn't the formats and approaches to a specific goal. The problem is in the lack of consistency. It seems that once we've tried one thing for a period of time, before you know it, we're off to something different, or we just quit altogether.

The universal principle to discipline that achieves results is consistency. A steady drip of water in one concentrated place will drill a hole in a rock over time.

Where is the determination to pay the price? Longevity should be the goal and sacrifice and self-discipline should be the price. You'll never get authentic results with imitation efforts. You didn't wake up this morning and realize you're overweight, your bank account is depleted, and your marriage is on the rocks. If this is the case, these situations are results of poor habits over time. Good or bad, these habits have created our culture. To break free from them and to see lasting significant change will require consistent daily steps over a significant season of time. Change will not happen overnight.

Where do you find yourself right now? Are you satisfied with where you are? Are you content with the results of your efforts or lack of effort? Do you find yourself bouncing from one new craze to the next?

Are you ready to lock into simplicity and implement small practical steps and habits consistently over time? I'm not talking about a fad or diet—I'm talking about a lifestyle.

Change of thoughts will produce change of feelings. Changed feelings will produce changed behavior. Changed behavior will produce better habits, and better habits will generate a healthier lifestyle. It all begins with how you are willing to see and think … consistently.

Character Does Count

Character is who we truly are on the inside. It's not our personality or the image we portray to the world. It's who we are when no one else is looking. Our truest self is defined by what we would do if there were no consequences.

There are those who would sacrifice character to cheat the system despite the consequences, only to find out in the end the system can't be cheated. There is no shortcut.

At the end of the day, character matters. It matters because it is the link to some things that are otherwise nonexistent. The virtues I mentioned earlier can only be authentically generated out of true character. Purity of heart cannot be faked. Intimacy is what it is. If you've experienced it, you understand this. The greatest level of intimacy can only be discovered through the deepest purity. Your integrity is worth everything you have to invest to maintain it. Again, it is not perfection. It is pursuit. It is intentional awareness of the state of the heart along with a holy guard against intruders.

Above all else, guard your heart, for everything you do flows from it. (Proverbs 4:23)

It does not matter how talented or educated you are, or how much money you may have. If you don't have character, you have nothing.

Attitude Determines Altitude

When I was growing up, I sometimes needed what parents commonly called an "attitude adjustment." Children can go from happy to cranky in mere seconds when they don't get their way, can't they? And many people undoubtedly carry this behavior into adulthood, some more than others depending on how it was managed during childhood.

Attitude is the guiding force that dictates everything from our quality of life to determining our success. Attitude determines altitude. Attitude is how I'm choosing to see things. I can potentially be in the worst of circumstances but maintain the most positive attitude. Attitude can defy odds and circumstances. It might not change the reality, but it can dramatically alter its impact. A positive attitude is the willful refusal to accept negativity as a state of being or an outcome. The only thing a negative attitude can accomplish is a worse outcome. If I am up against a challenge and have a negative attitude, the chances that my circumstance will become worse is greater than if I remain positive. Positivity is not "mind over matter." It is a decision to stay focused on what could be instead of what is.

Any successful athlete will tell you that mental conditioning in training is vital to winning. I love to watch Tiger Woods in a tournament. Like him or not, you cannot deny his mental discipline. He has almost mastered the ability to stay focused and not become distracted by anything, not even score.

Success in anything begins with a mindset. If you are going to win, you need to think like a winner. It's the mentality that makes or breaks the outcome of our circumstances.

Attitudes are also highly contagious. Good or bad, people catch them. Negativity and positivity are energies.

If I continue to walk with my head down, I will inevitably bump into something. With my head up and eyes focused on where I'm headed, I can see beyond what is directly in front of me. I think so often our heads are bowed in defeat from the continual badgering of negativity. We continue to walk, but because our eyes are downcast, we can't see far enough ahead to avoid hitting another obstacle, which only compounds the intensity of the situation.

Pick your head up. Stay focused. Don't become inoculated with a bad attitude. Stay away from toxic people who refuse to get their head out of the sand. Find a group of champions who will pour life into you. Find a consistent community of life-giving people until hope is all you see, and then share it with someone else.

Cultivating Gratitude

One of the most effective ways to maintain a positive attitude is to embrace a mindset of gratitude. Gratitude is a mindset that is cultivated through a disciplined thought life. It's all about where you continuously decide to keep your focus. If you're reading this, then you are alive, and that in itself is a reason to be grateful.

While we are still functioning, we have the will and authority to shape the life we desire. In order to do this, we must have a perspective that allows us to see the blessing of every opportunity. As long as time continues to move forward, we have the ability to make another decision that will propel us into the destiny of our dream and purpose. The only effective way to do this is to maintain a continual appreciation for what brought us to the place we are today. Never allow what you don't have to hijack the joy and value of what you do have. Life is not about the "haves" and "have nots." I reject the notion that everything in life revolves around chance. I do not believe in luck. I do not believe in karma. I believe in the powerful demonstration of virtues that construct an authentic and unshakable soul.

Gratitude is energy. Therefore, it is energizing. The one thing that makes the difference is our focus. Everyone has a story. That story consists of both the failures and the victories. If we get fixated on the negative, that's where we'll remain. We must choose to maintain a relentless focus on the victories. This is life-giving. Celebrate what you have. If you have little, celebrate that. Amounts are relative. Be grateful for it and you will receive more. Gratitude is the gateway to abundance.

Connected to the Source

In reference to the triune makeup of humanity, the spiritual component of the three must maintain connectivity with its source. The vehicle through which this takes place is prayer.

There are many misconceptions and misunderstandings about what prayer is and how to effectively pray. Once again, my resistance to complexity brings me back to stressing the simplicity of what's been made an overcomplicated subject.

Prayer is simply our spiritual communication with the Creator of the Universe. We are created in his image so there's never going to be anything about us that he doesn't understand.

Some have contrived elaborate, and unnecessary, rituals to reach him. I used to chuckle as a child when I would hear people attempt to pray in King James vernacular. "Hither and thither" and "thee" and "thou" were thrown around throughout the prayer in seeming attempts to make an impression on the "Big Man." It's sad to me when people think we can only connect with God if we impress him, as if our excellence of speech and disposition is what will grab his attention. It's absurd when you think about it.

God created us for relationship with him. It's really all he wants from us. In Genesis, it is clear that Adam and God walked and talked together every day. It was the primary reason why Adam was created.

Please don't misunderstand me. I believe in humility and reverence before God, but there is a difference between reverence and inferiority. I also believe in a healthy fear of God but believe there is a difference between healthy fear and intimidation.

There are a number of ways we can communicate with God. We can meditate. We can read his Word and listen as he speaks through the Scriptures. We can simply talk to him as a friend.

I don't know any elaborate prayers. My prayers are simple and sincere. I don't beg, plead, pander, or grovel. As a matter of fact, I rarely ask for anything. I'm not against asking, but most of what I need has already been promised to me, so I just thank God for it and declare it so. I've heard too many people pray for things that have already been given to them as a son or daughter of God.

My daily prayer might go something like this: "God, I thank you that I am blessed, secure, protected, and provided for today. I thank you that doors of opportunity are opening on my behalf." This prayer consists of more than just wishes and personal desires. This reflects the heart of God. He wants me to win. He gets pleasure when I succeed.

Again, simplicity with authenticity is the key. You don't need to scream at God to get his attention. This daily spiritual discipline is the bedrock of life itself. This component of our existence is what keeps us keyed into the source of life itself. It is a privilege to know the sovereign God through prayer.

I have watched how prayer has dramatically changed the complexion of my relationships over the years, beginning with my wife. I distinctly remember when the arguments between us began to diminish. I began to make a daily habit of walking over to her bedside and praying over her when I woke up every morning while she was still sleeping. Again, I don't ask God for anything. I speak everything he has already promised over her life. I thank him that she is blessed, protected, and provided for. I thank him for filling her with joy and favor.

If you don't already do this for your spouse, I encourage you to try it. I promise it has the power to transform your attitude toward your spouse. In our marriage, arguments began to die because I couldn't step out of the character of blessing her. I couldn't bring myself to invest in the time to bless her and then turn right around to curse her.

This was the intention when God created husband and wife. A marriage is a spiritual relationship, and when there is no spiritual connection to God who is the source, there can be no unity in the marriage relationship.

It's the same with my children. When I learned that if I prayed for them half as much as I complained about what they were doing wrong, things began to change—mostly my own attitude toward them. As a parent, I've come to realize that so often what we despise in our children is what we hate in ourselves. Some parents essentially spend their life confronting and correcting the things in their children that they never conquered in themselves.

The powerful thing about prayer is that it exposes things in us that might not otherwise be exposed. When things are exposed, we are then given the opportunity to confront and grow.

Freedom in Forgiveness

An essential part of prayer is forgiveness. When we approach God in prayer, we should express a humility with a concession of wrongs and offenses. As we seek forgiveness, we should be willing to forgive others before it becomes a stronghold in our life. Unforgiveness is a silent killer. It masquerades as an appeasement to the hurt administered by our enemies, but in reality, it is like continually drinking saltwater when you're dehydrated. Eventually, you die of dehydration even as you become thirstier. It's been said that unforgiveness is like drinking poison and expecting the other person to die.

When we learn to forgive, we learn to be truly free. It is one of the toughest lessons for humans to learn. We hold on to past hurts, offenses, and betrayals, foolishly thinking we can somehow fix, change, or rearrange the impact and pain, only to discover the dead end of torment. When I choose not to forgive, I am choosing to wallow in the abyss of deadlock, at the expense of my purpose and destiny. No new progress will be made as long as I continue to indulge in the façade of self-gratifying bitterness.

When we forgive someone who has hurt us, we are not excusing the wrong or denying the pain. We are simply releasing ourselves from the responsibility of managing a weight we were never created to carry. Forgiveness is not a feeling, but a decision, a choice, and a resolve.

It has been scientifically and medically proven that an individual who holds on to unforgiveness is consequently affected spiritually, emotionally, and even physically. Letting go and releasing hurt will literally improve your quality of life.

So, how do we forgive? I am going to give you some practical perspective as it relates to the act of forgiveness. I believe the first step is to resolve in your soul and spirit that revenge never produces a good result. Seeking to make someone suffer for what they did to you only keeps you in the victim position. Vengeance is a never-ending battle. At some level, we are all capable of inflicting suffering and pain on someone.

I have a mantra that I live by: "Just because I can doesn't mean I should." Our anger will often impair our perspective on what we could do versus what we should do. We should never act out of an elevated emotional state. Rarely does anything good come out of heightened emotions.

Next, you need to resolve who is in ultimate control of your wellbeing and destiny. I believe we get out of hand many times because we downsize the magnitude of God's creative power and resources. We think that if we don't repay the one who has hurt us, we've given them the upper hand. This couldn't be further from the truth. Know this: so much of what happens in our life is a test. Life is not about what happens to us, but how we respond to it. We cannot control most of what happens around us, but we can control our response to it. God is ultimately in control of it all. We must continue to keep trusting him with every situation. The moment we try to take control, we're putting faith in ourselves instead of God. True forgiveness is possible when we remain focused on the fact that God, not the person who has wronged us, has the ultimate authority over our life purpose and wellbeing. He will handle the rest. If the Creator of the Universe is for me—and he is—what does it matter who is against me?

The third step is to overcome evil with good. You may have heard it said that "only hurt people hurt people." This step is a bit tougher because it requires an empathy for your adversary. Yes, in spite of the severity of the pain, we should always seek to understand the reason behind the blow from our enemy. The majority of the people who are hurtful and hateful are battling with struggles of their own. There is a story behind every person that we know nothing about. When I am quick to judge and condemn others, I am essentially revealing an area of my own heart that is not healed. Whenever I seek revenge on my perpetrator, I am revealing unresolved hurt in my own life.

We've all hurt someone, either intentionally, unintentionally, or both. We tend to judge the actions of others more harshly than our own actions. I am not making excuses for undeserved actions as much as I am seeking to help us understand an important biblical principle:

> *Do not repay anyone evil for evil. Be careful to do what is right in the eyes of everyone. If it is possible, as far as it depends on you, live at peace with everyone. Do not take revenge, my dear friends, but leave room for God's wrath, for it is written: "It is mine to avenge; I will repay," says the Lord.*
>
> *On the contrary: If your enemy is hungry, feed him; if he is thirsty, give him something to drink. In doing this, you will heap burning coals on his head.*
>
> *Do not be overcome by evil, but overcome evil with good. (Romans 12:17-21)*

This brings forgiveness to an entirely new level. Not only should we forgive, but we should also bless those who have wronged us. For this to happen, the depth of your heart must always be greater than the size of your ego.

Building Intentional Relationships

There are so many things within the context of relationships that are central to everything in our lives. Success in our relationships is where it all begins. If we fail at relationships, every area of our life suffers.

We've all witnessed, and many have experienced, the heartbreak and grief of a shattered relationship. A bitter divorce is quite possibly the deepest grief a human can feel. I have performed numerous funeral ceremonies in my lifetime. The loss of a loved one is a traumatic grief, but it does not compare to that of a bitter divorce. The grave brings closure and finality with it. The divorce holds no closure other than the certificate of divorce, as life continues to go on.

Relationships are the epicenter of heartbreak, and the predominant link to completion.

It is often said, "The rise and fall of everything is leadership." I contend that leadership is important in every human situation. However, when you place the highest emphasis on leadership without its essential counterpart—relationship—you have nothing. Leadership without relationship is incomplete. Leadership without relationship will only create motion without emotion.

I fear that in an attempt to emphasize the significance of taking charge, being the initiator of constructive change, and ability to delegate, many prominent communicators and authors have either forgotten, or avoided the emphasis and necessity of the virtues that complete the composition of a true leader. Just because an individual knows how to move things forward and get stuff done does not make them a leader.

As a parent, I have the will and authority to lead my home. I can make the rules and enforce them if necessary. I can even get things done and make things happen within the context of the vision for my family. However, if I model and exhibit that version of leadership without cultivating relationship, I have created an environment of laws with consequences. This scenario will only erode my ability to authentically connect to my family in a manner that will generate followership out of love, honor, and respect. Relationships build the bridge of trust that will carry the weight of truth.

Relationship trumps leadership. I cannot lead well until and unless I can relate. My effectiveness as a leader is ultimately dependent upon my ability to relate and provide empathy and nurturing to those under my influence of leadership. Not just command, order, and activate. Otherwise, I am just a dictator who is legislating and enforcing rules and policies. Our most meaningful and productive leadership acumen can only be generated through the nurturing and cultivation of purposeful, deep relationships.

The entire reason for Jesus coming to this earth was to build the bridge for the relationship between God and mankind. It is clear that God values relationship above all else.

I believe the current condition of our world today is due to the breakdown of relationships. One might argue the chaos is due to lack of leadership. I wouldn't completely disagree, but I would ask you to take a close look at the condition of relationships in our world right now. I have personally never witnessed such divisiveness, contention, and hatred. I'm not talking about surface relationships or social media. I'm talking about families who are no longer speaking to one another because of contrasting political and world views. In that case, which do you think is most critical, leadership or relationship? Where is the most damage being done? It's in relationships, which is what is closest to the heart of God.

You can have relationship without leadership, but you cannot have effective leadership without relationship.

Relationships are vital to human growth and development. We were never meant to live isolated from one another.

Every entity on the planet requires one thing for its survival, productivity, health, and growth—people. And beyond this, the one additional necessary component is relationships. Think about it. The prosperity of any business depends on human relationships. You can't generate revenue and sales without people, and people won't respond to anything they don't have an affinity to.

In the world of real estate, I always hear that the key to a successful real estate purchase is "location, location, location." When it comes to humanity, I'll go on record as saying that the key to a productive and fulfilled life is "relationship, relationship, relationship."

Take a moment right now to analyze the health of your relationships. What's missing?

Become intentional about prioritizing your relationships. Honor others even when you don't agree with them. Value people who are different from you. Bring healing to those who are hurting. Bring joy to those who are mourning. Return love when you've been hated. Don't seek revenge but seek to empathize. Together we stand. Divided we fall.

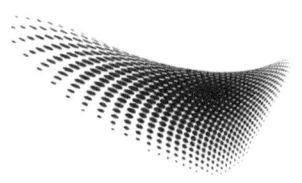

PART THREE
DEFYING YOUR LIMITATIONS EVERY DAY

DEFYING YOUR LIMITATIONS EVERY DAY

You Must Believe in You

Much of my early church culture frowned on any allusion to teaching self-confidence in fear that it would violate the biblical admonishment to deny yourself and place God and others above yourself. However, the biblical principles of humility and servanthood in no way suggest self-martyrdom or self-demoralization.

I was personally disillusioned by the idea that viewing myself as inferior and unworthy would make me more spiritual. I had a difficult time accepting the teaching that if I desired to do great things, dream, create, make money, and project confidence, God would condemn me for it.

The truth is, this is so far from the image and heart of the God that I have personally come to know. God is displeased with arrogance, haughtiness, self-serving and self-seeking temperaments, not with our desire to succeed.

Believing in yourself is critical to your effectiveness and productivity. What possible sense does it make for God to promise us his backing, blessings, and favor if he is just going to demoralize us for winning and prospering? As a father, I always celebrate the prosperity of my sons. I delight in their achievements. My expressed confidence in them is critical to their healthy development.

Insecurity, inferiority, and unworthiness have never accomplished anything worthwhile. I spent too much of my life with my head hung in shame. It is a miserable state of being.

You'll never see a successful athlete with a self-defeating attitude. An athlete who desires to win must have a winning disposition. This means that before the athlete wins on the field, he or she must win in the mind. Believing in yourself has to do with how you think. It is a "can do" mentality. If I believe I can, then I will. If I believe I can't, then I won't.

Philippians 4:13 tells us, "I can do all things through Christ who strengthens me."

What does this verse tell us that we need in order to accomplish what we set out to do? Of course, we need Christ. But Jesus is not going to take over and do everything for us. It must be done through him. This means I need the confidence, the grit, boldness, passion, dream, desire, and fortitude to know that I have everything I need, and through Christ there is nothing I can't accomplish.

I finally reached a place in my life where I realized that nothing great was ever going to happen until I kicked it into gear and started moving forward with a bold resolve. In addition, I began to believe that I did in fact deserve the reward of my results and that Christ deserves the glory and gratitude.

Let me firmly encourage you to begin to believe that you are created for a purpose. Stop hanging your head. Pick your chin up and walk with confidence. You must begin to see yourself as a winner. You are a champion and you should project it.

People will treat you the way you treat yourself. If you don't believe in yourself, why would you expect others to? You will attract the kind of person you are. What's even more sobering is that you will replicate who you are. The most effective way to attract successful people is to have a successful mindset and then carry yourself with confidence. Make yourself valuable. People are attracted to value. The opposite is also true. Misery loves company.

Allow your heart and mind to be transformed and carry yourself like you have a purpose and a mission. Stop walking around as though you are inferior to everyone around you. Discover the mystique that makes others wonder what you have. People are mesmerized by an individual who is composed with purpose, confidence, and resolve. Yes, they may still struggle with insecurity, but they have learned how to defy the gravitating and debilitating power of defeat. They have realized that just because we all will remain a work in progress until the day we die, doesn't mean we have to ever settle for mediocre.

Finding Your Tribe

You've heard it said, "You are becoming the company you keep." Show me your five closest relationships and I'll show you who you are becoming. Our influences shape us. We tend to absorb the ideals and values of those we are closest to. We "catch" behaviors, habits, and even menial views and philosophies.

Our associations have everything to do with our state of being. What good parent doesn't care about or monitor the friends and playmates of their own children? In fact, a parent can quickly determine the quality of influence by observing certain changes in their child's behavior following time with their friends.

Because of the power of influence that we as humans have over one another, it becomes imperative that we choose a community of relationships supportive of our aspirations and values.

Here is a list of things we need from those we interact with on a regular basis:

1.) **Value.** We need to surround ourselves with those who truly honor and value us. I personally refuse to spend time with people who are emotionally draining, especially if I have made every effort to pursue the health of the relationship. Your threshold may be different in what you allow and for how long. But, don't wait too long because toxicity can have far-reaching negative consequences. Toxic people are emotionally and mentally expensive in that they will drain everything they can from your account and then move on to those around you. I have discovered that I have the right to choose life-giving relationships with those who encourage, inspire, and genuinely value me as a person and also value my purpose. I am not looking for flattery and fluff. I just need relationships that are healthy enough to recognize the good, to value those virtues, and then to call it out of me. I don't need a group of people constantly criticizing me. If I allow that, I'll stay entrenched in my own imperfections. I choose to associate with people who will help me stay focused on my God-given attributes and gifts. I do my best to reciprocate this in relationships. I love to learn from the strengths of others. Don't hang with those who deplete you—hang with those who complete you.

2.) **Inspiration.** I believe there is a difference between motivation and inspiration. I believe that motivation pushes us, and inspiration pulls us. Motivation is an external compelling force while inspiration is an inner conviction and, for me, is a more sustaining force. People who have a story that has taken them from tragedy to triumph are inspirational. I need those stories. I'm talking about stories that cause something on the inside of you to leap. Stories with uncommon grit—relentless tenacity with a refusal to quit. I need to be around these people. I also need to be one of these people. My greatest likelihood of becoming my best self depends on my willingness and intentionality to spend time with others who are also driven to do so.

3.) **Support.** We need a few people in our lives who are committed to us unconditionally. This means an "any time and any place" type of commitment. I have known a few people in my lifetime who have said it, but who didn't really mean it. You are likely familiar with these people, too. Maybe they mean well but have no follow through.

When I was in my 30s, I served as a youth pastor. A father of one of the students in my group would tell me repeatedly how committed he was to the success of the youth ministry. Every time I saw him, he would remind me, "Anything you need, all you have to do is ask." One day, I decided to take him up on his offer. Our youth group was taking a trip and needed a good camera to take pictures. I knew that he owned one and I politely asked him if we could borrow the camera, assuring him that not only was the photographer trustworthy, but the camera would not leave her hands. He turned me down without hesitation. It was clear that what he meant by "anything" meant anything that didn't require sacrifice on his part. If there were conditions involved, maybe he should have said, "anything except…"

Find some people who you can build strong trust and equity with, and those people will be willing to be there for you unconditionally.

4.) **Loyalty.** We need people in our lives who know the worst about us but choose to see the best and speak the best. People who know many of your secrets and short-comings but understand the power and integrity of confidentiality. Sounds as though I'm describing a type of friendship that doesn't exist, doesn't it? They're out there, but they just have to be tested. I don't trust people who tell me other people's secrets. When someone is talking about someone else to you, rest assured they are talking about you to someone else. This is a character problem. It is a weakness that you cannot afford to subject yourself to. As soon as I hear an individual begin tearing down someone else, I become gravely concerned. Not only is gossip immature, but it is rooted in jealousy, envy, insecurity, and malice. Run from this. Avoid it at all costs. It is counterproductive and destructive. Search for and lock into those relationships that may be a work in progress but are authentic, fulfilling, and constant.

The Most Difficult Person
You'll Ever Lead – You

The key to any positive change begins with a mind shift. The quickest and most effective way to experience an authentic mind shift is to become self-aware. This is when and where self-leadership begins.

The most difficult leadership role we will ever have will be to lead the person in the mirror. The effectiveness with which we self-lead will determine our level of effectiveness in leading others.

Authentic self-leadership is one of the truest and toughest tests a human will endure. It is a continual process of removing anything from our lives that is contrary to the virtues exhibited and lived out in the life of Jesus.

As we consider what we expect of others, we must also self-evaluate to determine whether these virtues are evident in our own lives. This is called humility. The evidence of these virtues becomes apparent over time.

Want to know if you're leading yourself well? Walk through this analysis with me—How do you react to hate? How do you respond to your critic? What do you sound like on a phone call with a difficult person? How do you behave in traffic? (Ouch. That hits most of us right between the eyes.)

Effective self-leadership doesn't deny you the negative emotion of a moment; it just denies you the right to negatively respond and react. It doesn't deny us the opportunity to be tempted, just the permission to indulge. Again, we are works in progress. I believe the world is disheartened by the dichotomy of leaders speaking truth and character publicly and attempting to lead others toward virtues and behaviors they haven't mastered privately in themselves. The objective of self-leadership is to consistently and intentionally cultivate the habits and virtues in our individual private lives that ultimately generate and exhibit the type of character that purely stands out in our public life. This creates lasting change. And when transformation happens personally, it translates publicly.

Effective self-leadership cannot happen without authentic self-awareness, which again is where the value of relationships comes in. This will also mean allowing certain trusted friends and mentors to speak truth into our lives. The Bible gives several references to this kind of accountability:

Proverbs 27:17 says, "As iron sharpens iron, so one person sharpens another."

And in verses five and six of the same chapter: "Better is open rebuke than hidden love. Wounds from a friend can be trusted, but an enemy multiplies kisses."

The images portrayed in these verses are of authentic, loving truth. Many will say they welcome this in their life, but when the truth is difficult to hear, they become selective about what they will receive depending on how it affects their comfort level.

Who is qualified to be iron in my life? First, my spouse has unrestricted liberty to call me out, and she does. Now, please understand, this is not permission to berate and demoralize me. This can only happen in a life-giving way when two people are in total unity in a deep trusted relationship.

My immediate family members have the right to speak into my life. Beyond this, I have a few close and trusted friends who have a level of permission to do the same. This keeps me in check. Left exclusively to ourselves we will self-destruct.

Self-awareness is a genuine reality check but isn't ultimately effective without those who are committed to helping you become the very best version of you. True maturity happens when we can receive the truth in love and then process and implement the necessary adjustments.

I am not the person today that I was destined to become as a child. I am also not the person today that I was becoming as a young adult. I am not the man I used to be years ago, and I am not even the man I was yesterday. My pursuit and my passion every day is to be a better leader, a better husband, a better father, and a better grandfather than I was the day before. It's a daily pursuit that looks ahead and not behind. I don't waste time hung up on the mistakes and failures of yesterday because I'm more focused on how to improve for tomorrow.

Slowing Down to Self-Replenish

With all the busyness of life's demands, and the stress that goes with it, do you ever take time for yourself? I often come across individuals who are exhausted and depleted, never allocating any margin for self-rejuvenation. It's all give, give, give and go, go, go.

It has been said, "If your output exceeds your intake, your upkeep will be your downfall."

So many great and gifted people have no boundaries to keep them from overextending and overtaxing their body, mind, and spirit. Many of us don't understand the power of "no," and the rest of us don't know how to honor human capacity.

None can compare to the potential and performance of the human body. However, it will not endure long-term abuse without severe consequences. If you take great care of your body, it will take ultimate care of your assignments and responsibilities. Many of us know how to be busy but are disappointed when we see very little results from our obdurate efforts. We must wisely steward and maximize our time, efforts, and energy. The only way this will happen is to be intentional about what we do, how we do it, when we do it, and for how long.

The big idea of life is to make a difference in the world we live in. Be the change. Create impact. You cannot do this effectively in a depleted state. What are we told during the review of the safety regulations before every flight takes off? Secure your oxygen mask first. What good are you to anyone else if you can't breathe? The same applies in life. Your effectiveness in others is dependent on the care for yourself. You're only as good to others as your own wellbeing. You cannot give away what you do not have.

Establishing Healthy Habits

There are countless philosophies for adopting and implementing healthy habits. I'm not questioning their validity as much as I am challenging their necessity. Much of the self-help market is overrated and overcomplicated. It seems to me that marketers have tried to creatively manipulate the average human with complexity-based principles in hopes of making discipline seem easier to get people motivated enough to buy into something that will hopefully generate change. It sounds amazing and easy so it must work, we think.

There is an astounding simplicity to my methodology and philosophy. I believe that if you really want it, you'll go for it. We don't always pursue what we truly need. However, we always go after what we want.

As a result of being a life coach and mentor, whenever I am assisting someone to experience life change, I always take them through a process of defining and resolving their "why." Why is this important to you? Why are you doing this? I do not believe we can ever get true and lasting results from our extended goals and endeavors if we don't resolve the deepest reason and purpose for pursuing the end result.

Here is the formula for that philosophy once the "why" has been sealed: desire + strategy + discipline + consistency = results.

The only other addition is a continual visit and reminder of the "why."

In its simplest context, it means that if you really have a desire to see results and change, you'll put a plan together, discipline yourself to the plan, stick to the plan consistently, and, over time, you'll get the desired results. Also, our strongest commitment should be to the journey—not the result. The process will generate the desired results over time if we're truly committed and consistent. If we obsess over the end result, we'll lose interest and momentum, and eventually abort the mission.

Habits are simply repeated actions over time.

In my own life, if I really want something, I will do my thorough research in order to find out the best plan and strategy. After that, I am going to work the plan and tweak it as needed, but I will not relent until I see the finished product. Those who know me well will tell you I am like a mule when it comes to implementation. I will commit until the bloody end. My "why" is anchored deep. I have been called "fanatic," "health nut," and "extreme." However, some of these same critics have later asked my advice on how to accomplish some of the very things in their own life they'd previously criticized in mine.

I have been committed to physical fitness for most of my life. Part of what drove me to this was a skepticism of diets and health fads. I'm so disheartened when I see an individual lose an enormous amount of weight, only to gain it all back six months later. How does this happen? Because they didn't adopt the habits that helped them achieve the results. Habits are intentional actions that have potential and power to produce results. The caveat is that once the habit stops, so do the results. A habit is only as powerful as its activity.

You must also identify and guard against distractions. You can have passion and a plan, but if you allow distractions to sidetrack you, you will never reach your goal. Repeated distractions will cause you to lose your focus and eventually erode your desire, costing you greatly. Sadly, you find yourself disheartened and back to square one. I have wasted many workouts at the gym due to engagement in a conversation that could have and should have happened at a different time and place. We must learn how to guard what we have sanctioned sacred.

Habits are happening every day either by default or intentionality. We're either making things happen or allowing things to happen. Either way, the result is the difference between a good and healthy habit, or a bad and destructive one.

So, how must one begin new and healthy habits? My practice is to implement a new habit as often as possible. As a personal rule, I like to incorporate a physical habit, a mental habit, and a spiritual habit simultaneously. Once again, I want to stress the connectivity between the body, soul, and spirit. I undoubtedly believe that these three components are performing best when they are performing in symphony. Therefore, for example, if I were going to implement the habit of honoring others more, I would practice verbally expressing honor (physical), mentally thinking of ways to honor others (soul), and then incorporate more gratitude and thankfulness into my prayer time (spiritual). One physical, mental, and spiritual habit reinforced and aligned to be much more powerful and effective.

When we initiate a new habit, it is also important that we get rid of an old one. If I am committed to start exercising, I can't continue to make poor diet choices. I also cannot continue to think the same way. If I am going to see lasting results, I must be committed to change in every way to create a new lifestyle.

If we can change our thinking, our values will change. This change of values will transform our habits. Habits, over a period of time, will translate into a lifestyle. If you desire life change, you must create the necessary lifestyle to reinforce the change. Otherwise, you wind up on a rollercoaster of results.

Where are you stuck? Do you have those in your life who have permission to speak the truth to you? If so, do you receive it?

The Joy of Generosity

To truly give is to lose authority and control over the gift. We used to call this "with no strings attached." That's a rare concept these days, isn't it?

The ultimate spirit of giving is found in John 3:16-17:

> *For God so loved the world that he gave his one and only Son, that whoever believes in him shall not perish but have*

eternal life. For God did not send his Son into the world to condemn the world, but to save the world through him.

God gave his only Son for you and for me, unconditionally with no strings attached. Some may argue that he ultimately wants our devotion in return. To that I would say, he came to give us life. No matter how you spin it, you still come out winning.

This giving nature is in our spiritual DNA. Selfishness exists, but even within the most selfish individual there is an instinctive desire to give. Why? Because we are created in the image of the ultimate giver.

There is no denying that when we give, something miraculous takes place. Not just for us, but for the individual who receives the gift. We are never more like God than when we give. Within the heart of true giving is love, and God is love.

The very expression of giving moves us beyond ourselves. It forces us to see beyond our own necessities. Selfishness is the instinct of our humanity. We strive and toil most of our lives to self-educate and acquire degrees that will land us the high-income jobs, just so we can indulge in a sense of security that leads us to believe that if we have enough, we're insulated from lack. This is backwards thinking. The greatest security is derived through giving. There is a law of reciprocation that goes into effect the moment we authenticate this powerful principle in our life. The surest way to securely posture your future and the future of your children and grandchildren is to become a "no strings attached" giver.

If you want to break through some of life's greatest challenges and limitations, establish the principle of consistent giving. You don't "give to get." However, you are the number one recipient of your giving because, as we learn in Scripture, it is more blessed to give than to receive. I am always looking for opportunities to give, and not just financially, but with all of my resources.

Giving frees the soul, it liberates the spirit, and releases unstoppable blessings.

I believe that giving reinforces gratitude. Gratitude is the heart of giving. We give because we are grateful and because we desire someone else's life to become enriched with what we have experienced. The attitude of gratitude inspires our purpose, shapes our perspective, and sharpens our spirit.

Selfishness, greed, and egotism are destructive forces that will take root in our soul if we're not careful. They lie to us with logic that says that if we have more money, then we have more power, and with more power comes more control. This is representative of the economy of humanity. However, the economy of heaven exhibits the exact opposite.

> *For whoever wants to save their life will lose it, but whoever loses their life for me will find it. (Matthew 16:25)*

I will always treasure this precious quote by Christian missionary Jim Elliot: "He is no fool who gives what he cannot keep to gain that which he cannot lose."

Experience the ultimate joy. Be a giver. How do you become a giver? Start by giving something. I will guarantee you that once you begin to experience the joy of giving, you'll look for more opportunities to give. It will change your life. It will change your perspective. Giving will revolutionize your heart. Giving will break you free from stigmas and growth barriers you never even knew existed in your life.

The Recipe for Defying Limitations

You may have a mother or grandma who can cook like nobody's business. If so, you know that most good cooks keep the recipes to their signature dishes a secret.

Occasionally, we discover people who seem to have a secret recipe to a certain area of success in life. Sometimes they will hold on to it for fear they won't get deserved credit for the formula. Fortunately, this way of thinking has improved over the years and now most thriving organizations will freely share information in an effort to help.

I am an organizational consultant and personal life coach. I have devoted my entire life to helping others succeed. I experience no greater joy than helping an individual shatter their personal limitations and conquer their fears, or to receive an invitation to sit at the table with the leadership of an organization and provide perspective and insight that can help produce results. My personal mission is to help as many people as I can to become the very best version of themselves. The objective of this book is to provide perspective, philosophies, and tools to revolutionize your thinking and inspire you to break free from average. Whenever you win, I win. My life purpose is to give my life away. The more that I give, the more that will be given. I'm not just giving to you, but I'm also giving through you. If you will receive what has been given to you, and then freely give it to someone else, you will have discovered the meaning of life.

I would like to give you the recipe that helps me to daily defy my limitations. This recipe is not going to create a dish that satisfies everyone's tastebuds. It will simply serve as a template. Tweak it. Make it your own. Personalize it to fit your season of life. The premise is a foundational launching pad. The idea is to present something that you can use to build upon.

First, I believe that every human being must have personal written core values. Again, your values are derivatives of what you believe. What you believe will dictate what you value. Values will determine how you behave. We enter businesses and organizations all the time that have core values plastered on almost every wall of the organization. If it is significant for the organization, why wouldn't it be significant for the individuals who are part of the organization?

As you begin to think about this and begin the process of contriving your own personal core values, don't just think about what is important to you now, but also what you want to be important to you moving forward.

Writing personal core values will keep your priorities in the forefront of your life, influencing your most detailed actions. They will also serve to remind you of what you will not compromise. The end goal is to have a list of values that reinforce the kind of character virtues you wish to develop.

How many core values should you end up with? Too few and you won't capture all the unique dimensions of your being. Too many and you'll forget them or won't take advantage of them. A list of no more than seven and no less than three is ideal.

There are many resources on the internet that will provide even more insight as to how to effectively contrive your personal core values. My suggestion would be for you to begin at the end. That's right—the end of your life. Ask yourself what you would like for people to say about you at your funeral and begin cultivating those attributes and virtues right now.

You must prioritize what you value over what is easy and ordinary. Also, know that once you have adopted a list of personal core values, they may change over the course of your life as you grow and develop.

Here are my current personal core values:

- I push through pressure.
Pressure reveals weakness, which creates opportunities for growth.
- I am the master of my emotions.
Feelings aren't always reality. I am in full control.
- I prioritize "we" over "me."
Serve others first.
- Purity is power.
Decisions made in private will project in public. Purity brings intimacy and intimacy brings power.
- I don't compete, I win.
Competitive people lose, but winners win.
- Comparison is the intruder of my best self.
When I focus on becoming my best self, my best gets better.

Once again, these will likely evolve. These fit perfectly into my current season of life. The winds of change will come, and I will adjust the sails accordingly.

Another ingredient to the recipe for success is a list of statements that affirm my identity. These are my personal daily declarations. Why are declarations important? I believe our most effective responses are to what we hear repeatedly. Repetition is an amazing developer. Also, if you want to overcome fear (and we all deal with fear) your affirming declarations will combat fear and build your faith and confidence. How? Because Romans 10:17 tells us that faith comes through hearing. If you speak life-giving words, you'll be the first to hear them and they will produce faith inside of you.

Declarations are mere reinforcements to your identity and purpose. I speak these out loud every day:

- I am a son of God.
- Life and death are in my tongue.
- I am living in my God-given purpose.
- I am secure in who I am and who God says I am.
- My life is making a difference.
- My mind is sharp, my body is healthy, my spirit is alive.
- I am blessed and have favor with God and man.
- There is more potential in me.
- I will never give up or be defeated.

Feel free to use these if they are fitting. If not, make your own. What is most important is the habit and repetition of declaring them daily.

The final ingredient is my own personal morning ritual. I hope this will serve as a guide that will enable you to shape your own productive and life-giving daily routine:

- Prayer
- Bible Reading
- Book Reading
- Declarations
- Core Values
- Journaling
- Exercise

Time for each of these is discretionary and varies. Typically, I spend a total of one hour daily (minus gym time).

You can do this. Don't allow time and distraction to dictate whether you implement these critical components to your daily life. I have discovered that I will make time for what I really desire. If I am hungry, I will find food and the time to eat. It has been said, "If you truly desire something, you'll find a way–if you don't, you'll find an excuse."

I encourage you to try this recipe for yourself. I think you'll be amazed at how it will inspire and help you grow and develop in the pursuit of your purpose.

My Personal Mission

As important as I believe it is to have personal values and declarations, I believe it is just as critical to know your personal mission. A personal mission is a compilation of your passion, your gifts, and your calling. It's not just what you're good at, but it's also what fulfills you. It's what you're effective at doing.

As I mentioned earlier, my personal mission is to help as many people as possible become the best version of themselves. This is fulfilling for me because it is what my passions and gifts contribute to the world.

What about you? Why are you here? What were you made for? What are you called to do?

You were not placed on this earth for yourself alone. You were made to contribute to the betterment of others. Then, and only then, will you discover the meaning and purpose of living.

Controlling Only What You Can Control

It goes without saying that much of our lives is spent worrying about things we cannot change and trying to control things we have no control over.

Let's get very practical. I cannot control what other people do. I can, however, control my response to it. I have full control over my attitude, my thoughts, emotions, my behavior, and most importantly, my relationship with God. This is really what's most important.

It is disparaging to watch the hate-filled opinions blasted across social media that produce nothing more than factions and division. These days people will destroy a relationship to win an argument. Is it really worth it? Even if you win the argument, what did you really accomplish?

I love what Andy Stanley said: "Jesus did not come to earth to make a point. He came to make a difference."

Remaining focused on what we can control provides us the cutting edge to win in life. We must let go of what we cannot change to fight for what we can.

I am most effective when I am completely devoted to my God-given purpose and assignment. Everything else is a waste of time and energy. We can still have profound influence on things outside of our control and maintain the integrity of our purpose regardless of the outcome.

At the end of our lives, what do we really want to be known for? You do have control over the legacy you're creating each and every day. Invest your energy into things that matter.

In retrospect, I've wasted too much time and energy on things that I could not change. What's worse is, many of the causes didn't really matter.

Not everyone's drama needs to become yours. Ask yourself if your involvement will make a difference. And, more specifically, what difference would that be? I've heard too many stories of individuals who stubbornly remained in a relationship because they were convinced that they could change the person. Again, we have every right to be influencers. However, we must be smart and strategic as to how, when, and for how long. The rest is out of our control.

True and lasting peace comes with resolving what you can and cannot control. I am learning to redirect my thoughts from the worry and anxiety that comes from trying to maneuver a way to control a situation that, in the end, I won't be able to change. When a worrisome thought enters my mind, I'm learning to run an analysis through a series of questions: Is there anything I can do about this situation? If so, what? If not, I intentionally, strategically, and purposefully redirect my thoughts to something life-giving and uplifting. It took some time and practice at first, but now I find that it works every single time.

Reversing the Curse of the Common

Throughout our life, we will experience things that will shake us and challenge the way we think.

Whenever major events take place in the world, we tend to pay attention. I'll never forget where I was on September 11, 2001. My immediate response was grief for the victims and families and anger toward the terrorists who had committed this atrocity. Then, I began to consider how this would affect me as an individual. Things and places that we had historically deemed safe weren't safe any longer. America as a country, and Americans as individuals, had to now adjust to this new normal. This one single event shook us right out of a mentality of comfort and complacency into a posture of awareness. We weren't just shaken but were awakened to a new reality.

As creatures of habit, we have a strong propensity to fall into apathetic ruts. We fall into the familiarity of our daily grind, not realizing we're just victims of a vicious cycle, until something jars our routine in a way that changes our perspective.

What about when someone close to us experiences tragedy? What typically happens is that once we navigate through the emotions of the event and our loved one's wellbeing, we begin to internalize. What about me? Could this happen to me? It often becomes a wakeup call to reflect on our own lives.

There came a time when I knew I had to reverse the curse of common if I wanted to experience lasting change. I had to break the bond of lethal ritual. I knew there was a better version of myself and I desperately needed to discover it. We may have been negatively shaped by our cultures of origin, but, as I hope you've come to understand over the course of this book, our thoughts, attitudes, and behaviors of yesterday do not have to be those of today. While I can never undo yesterday's decisions, I can change today's and get different and better results for tomorrow. Trajectories can be changed. Curses can be broken. Outcomes within our personal control and grasp can be determined.

What rut are you currently entrenched in? What familiar dysfunctions have you settled for? What would it take to shake you out of them? Let this be your wakeup call.

If you are reading this, you have a responsibility. If you are a single adult, you owe it to yourself at this stage of your life to assess now. Are you emotionally and spiritually healthy enough to attract healthy relationships, and, at some point, a healthy mate for life? Decide early and get the advantage.

If you are married and without children but are planning to grow your family, is your current state of marriage healthy and stable enough to provide the kind of culture that will instill wholesome emotions and attitudes in your future children? Will you repeat the cycle of generational dysfunction? Or, will you take hold of the now and make necessary changes for a better tomorrow?

No matter where you find yourself on your journey, it's never too late to change the trajectory of your future.

Your Next Step is a Step

There are times in life when we find ourselves in the clutches of debilitating indifference. It's that place we find ourselves when we know we need to make a move but don't know the first step to take. We lack strategy. And, to top it off, we can't seem to muster up the necessary motivation to get going. We're stuck. And our fear is that as the clock keeps ticking, we will look back in time only to discover we're in the same place and same condition.

Whatever state of quandary and indifference you are in right now, I have some news for you: nothing ever happens without motion. Everything is immobilized until and unless something moves. The eventual paralyzing impact of inactivity is much more devastating than stepping out, taking risks, and failing. We should never fear what will happen if we try, more than we fear what will happen if we don't. The eventual momentum achieved from the action to take risk will pay off in the long run.

We are born for greatness. Since the very beginning of time, we have all been commissioned to subdue the earth, be fruitful, and multiply. Every single thing in creation emulates this. The ultimate fulfillment in life comes when we are doing what we were created to do. Everything outside of that generates frustration, anxiety, and confusion—all of which are counterproductive to accomplishing great things and making a difference.

The greatest joy in life comes when an individual is willing to sacrifice safety, comfort, and familiarity in order to exist in an atmosphere of purpose, meaning, and productivity. Take a chance. Take a risk. Get your head out of the cloud of lies that is telling you to remain where you are, thinking that's where you'll be safest. Defy this mindset of mediocrity. You are made for more.

Pressure

There will always be times and seasons in our lives when circumstances push us to think differently. A life that is void of pressure will not have the opportunity to intersect with change and growth. There will be times when we are forced to an ultimatum. The pressure will be so great, and the mental and emotional turmoil will be so intense, that we will be presented with two options: quit or push forward.

This is where many will give up, and here are some reasons why:

1.) Individual identity is not solidified. This is an ongoing process. Your identity will be challenged continuously. Voices and activity around you will cause you to question who you are. More importantly, you'll doubt and second-guess your value and contribution to the world.

2.) Questionable trust. Your level of trust in God directly impacts your trust in his purpose for your life.

There came a point in my life when I realized that most of my efforts were spent trying to avoid pain and pressure. I think a lot of this is just human nature. We instinctively seek the path of least resistance. My "a-ha" moment was when I realized that pressure, fear, and emotional pain were opportunities—not problems. It was then I discovered the secret of boldly confronting my fear and opposition.

There are times when a ship at sea has no choice other than to steer into a storm. The ship must keep its bow pointing into the waves to plow through them safely, since a massive wave striking the ship's side could roll the vessel over and sink it. Wind and waves will try to turn the vessel and pushing against them requires forward momentum. We can potentially become a casualty of our own desire for safety. Playing it safe most often will cost us way more than just kissing the waves, so to speak. I have learned much more from pushing through my life's storms than I have trying to escape them. Now, please understand, I'm not a glutton for punishment. I don't storm chase, but, where I stand today, I'm not going to back down from one either. You will overcome your greatest fears, challenges, and obstacles by confronting them not avoiding them.

Also, understand there are many who will advise you to play it safe. The reason others give you fear-based advice

is because, in reality, they're projecting their own uncon-
quered fear.

Just Start

There will never be a better time to initiate change than
now. Procrastination will just compound the complexity and
frustration—not to mention the waste of more time. Nothing
exists outside of this moment. You have exclusive control
over the now. Not the past, not the future. Only now. Sometimes, the most profound thing you can do is to take one
step now. Even if you don't have a clear strategy yet, the
movement in the general direction of the goal will propel
you toward a simple accomplishment. This simple accomplishment just might be exactly what you need to begin
to feel like you have a worthy cause. Movement produces
momentum.

Some believe that taking the initial step toward a goal is
the most difficult part of the process. I disagree. I believe
it is the easiest part of achieving a goal. All it requires is
sheer will. The remainder of the process, in my opinion, will
be what will require the most commitment, discipline, and
focus. Nothing happens until you start. Nothing happens
unless you start.

Beginnings are exciting. Small beginnings, even more so.

The greatest emotional cancer in life is not failure—it is
regret. Failure is just an opportunity to learn. Failure turns
knowledge into wisdom. Regret is an antagonizing reminder
of what might have happened if only we had tried and tried
again. Regret replays disappointment. It paralyzes our faith
until we decide to get up, take a step, and continue to move
in a forward direction. I don't want to get to the end of my

life and regret missed opportunities.

I believe there are three common dream killers. The first is procrastination. We rationalize to ourselves that, when certain things are aligned, it will increase our chances to win. So, we wait. Think about how many times we say, "One day, I'll … (fill in the blank)."

As it relates to your personal growth and development, there can be no better time than now. Stop putting off what you know you should do today. Destroy the lurking thoughts of deferment. Eliminate excuses. Seize the moment. Get moving now.

The second dream killer is fear: fear of failure, fear of what others will think, fear of more responsibility. The only way to starve fear is to feed your faith, which requires daily, consistent contributions.

The third is laziness. I've often said, if poverty were a state, lazy would be the capital. Laziness isn't just lack of passion but lack of interest. If there is a component of human nature that we must all guard against, it is laziness. I don't know any successful people who are lazy, do you?

Your purpose is waiting. Your best self is yet to be discovered. Nothing happens until you make it happen. Take control. Make a decision. Draw a line in the sand. What are you waiting for? Is it worth allowing to hijack your dream? I don't think so.

Setting a Goal

Zig Ziglar once said, "If you aim at nothing, you will hit it every time." Generating hope is pointless if you don't have something to strive for. Our lives should be a list of mile-stones that include shattered ceilings, breakthroughs, discoveries, and victories. The zest of life is accomplishing a goal, and then setting the bar higher.

You can have a dream, but, without goals, it is nothing more than a fantasy. Our dream must be structured with strategies and deadlines.

I have always been a huge proponent of beginning at the end. Most of what I do begins with the end in mind, and then I work my way back. This book began with a big idea. The idea was to provide a resource in how to defy limitations in order to achieve purpose and fulfillment. This is what I would call the "what." Following the big idea, I began to think through the reason and value of this resource. This would be the "why." Then I began to map out a plan that would provide practical and insightful principles that, if implemented, could be life changing. This is the "how."

Adopting this simple formula into our aspirations could revolutionize our productivity and maximize our time and effectiveness. Not to mention, we would gradually see our dreams come to fruition.

Our goals should correlate with our overall life mission and purpose. Many of our daily activities are not contributing to a defined mission. We're all over the board. We're distracted so easily. We lose focus and, before you know it, our aspirations are caught up in the wind. We eventually abandon the mission for lack of context.

One of the first things I had to learn about being effective on social media as it relates to my career is to define my voice and my audience. Who am I? Who do I need to speak to? Once I resolved my passion, what I truly had a heart to do, and what I wanted to say, I was able to determine who my message should speak to. As an organizational health specialist, I speak to organizations who are experiencing issues with poor communication, lack of engagement, lack of value, and poor leadership development. That is my voice. If I begin to randomly sprinkle some political rhetoric, for example, into my social media posts, I'll confuse the audience. So, my goals complement the theme of my voice.

If you want to be effective in life, you'll need to learn alignment. Align your values, habits, and goals with your mission and dream. Don't compromise. Never negotiate. Remain on track. Stay focused. Your goals are benchmarks.

On my larger aspirations I will set a yearly goal, a quarterly goal, a monthly goal, and weekly goals. My daily goals will contribute to my weekly and monthly goals. When you set a goal, you immediately bring accountability into the equation. The problem with not setting goals is, because you have no benchmarks or deadlines, you are essentially giving yourself permission to procrastinate.

We let ourselves down way more than other people do. We love to blame others for our setbacks, but we are more responsible for them than anyone. We have the time and power to accomplish anything we set our mind and will to. We can either be our greatest commodity or our biggest obstacle.

Setting goals should be an organic component of our lives. If we truly desire to see results, we should establish a benchmark that will hold us accountable to progress.

If this is a new concept for you, start small. Think of something you've been wanting to get done, look at your calendar, set a reasonable timeline by which to get it done, and then build an action plan to get you to your deadline.

Managing Your Time

Speaking of deadlines, it is sobering to think about how quickly the clock moves. We hear it so often, but time flies. The older I get, the more I know it to be true.

When I was in my youth, I felt like time would go on forever. I never had one single thought of death. I couldn't imagine a life with children and grandchildren. It's not that I didn't want to, but I was so preoccupied with the present moment that the future just seemed vague and obscure to me. Age tends to teach us the value of time. Reflecting on the past can bring regret when we think of time wasted. We cannot recapture moments, days, and years.

We are only given one life, and we don't get a do-over. This is why we must make the moments we have today count. There is nothing more discouraging than a wasted day. How many days have you let slip by and asked, "Where did the time go and what did I get done?"

A wise person doesn't put things off assuming there will be another opportunity tomorrow. Maybe there will be. Maybe there won't. We are not guaranteed another breath. So, it begs the question, how are you stewarding your time? And how are you leveraging the time you have to make it count? Are you making progress? Are you setting and reaching your goals? Or, are you allowing the clock to dictate your schedule? Are you in command of the time you have within a twenty-four-hour window? What should you be responsibly working toward? What have you repeatedly procrastinated?

What will you do about it?

As important as it is to set goals, it is equally important to steward your time. How you steward your time will dictate what you achieve. If you squander time, you'll never master effectively achieving your goals. Time is on your side only if you honor, value, and respect it. Effective time management begins with allocating specificity to your day. We must take control of the time we have, or it will take control of us.

The Power of Change

No one will ever convince me that we are forever stuck with where we are and with what we have. I am living proof that any person can defy almost any odds. The thought of change is nothing until we make a decision.

We must perform a personal, uninterrupted analysis of our current situation and ask tough questions. Is where I currently am where I want to be? Is this what my life is supposed to be? Am I satisfied with my current levels of efficiency and effectiveness? Is there more for me? What price am I willing to pay for more? How long have I known that I haven't made progress? Why am I still sitting here?

Most aren't willing to step away from the familiar and comfortable because of fear. Fear is an illusion. It isn't real. It is a façade. It whispers negativity. It administers delusional paralysis. Fear's objective is to keep you insulated until you become isolated. If you are isolated long enough, you forfeit the voice of challenge until it eventually leaves you alone. When your enemy discovers your deepest fear, he'll leverage it to control you.

We are made for change. We are designed and equipped

for challenge. Our entire being is made for resistance. The power of change embodies the light of vision. New levels, new heights, new altitudes, and new rewards await. Change introduces a new season. Seasons are magical. Most everyone has a favorite season of the year. However, I think we can all agree that the change in the seasons is welcomed year after year. An entire year of any one of the four would be monotonous and unpleasant to say the least. I enjoy the transition from spring to summer. I love to see the blooms on the trees and the new fresh flowers beginning to sprout. I also have a swimming pool in my back yard that reminds me it won't be long before we're able to enjoy the cool soothing saltwater under the warm summer sun.

I'm thankful for life's changes and transitions. For with each, there is another opportunity to step into a greater, better, more powerful and rewarding stage of life.

The Bigger Picture

It can sometimes seem that life is a continual quest to solve a mystery. I've said before that life is a test. Not a test to determine whether we are fit or not, or even if we will make it to the end or not, but one much deeper than that. It's the kind of test that is set in place and designed to determine what and who we will ultimately become.

Many of the questions we all face from day to day will never be answered. Why is world hunger an issue? Why do good people suffer? Why are some people so cruel? Why do the atrocities of human trafficking, abuse, and murder exist? These are the questions that have the potential to limit us in the pursuit of our dreams. Unlike the heroism and acts of goodwill that give us hope in humanity and inspire us to forge ahead, the evils in our world can cause us to want to give up.

Life is a journey of setups and setbacks, mountaintops and valleys, and changing seasons. In the unknown of what we will face from day to day, we are confronted with another question: what and who will we trust?

We're living in a time when so many things in which we've placed our confidence have been shaken. In the last year alone, we've experienced record-breaking hurricanes and wildfires, rioting and destruction in the streets of our cities, one of the most divisive presidential elections in history, and a global pandemic that shut down our daily lives, businesses, and even our ability to gather in our sacred houses of worship.

What are we to do when everything we've placed our security in seems to be falling apart around us? What do we do when our human institutions, systems, and leaders fail us?

When the dust settles and we begin to see more clearly, we can fall into despair and hopelessness, or we can look confidently to the only Source who is worthy of our complete trust.

Money, fame, power, possessions, and government institutions are temporal. Even the most trustworthy people will fall short and disappoint us. At some point in all of our lives we will come to a crossroads, faced with a decision to continue striving in self-sufficiency, or surrendering to our Creator who has been patiently waiting for us all along.

Life is a continual battle between good and evil. Defying your limitations in pursuit of your purpose is ultimately about bringing light to a dark world. It's about becoming the person you were destined to be in order to bring goodness to the world around you.

I'm grateful to those who came before me and chose to push past hopelessness and defy the odds. I'm thankful for those who stood up to the challenges of their generation and took action.

While we may find ourselves discouraged and overwhelmed at times when we consider the problems in our world today, I want to remind you that you were created to be part of the solution. The impact you are destined to have in the world around you, begins inside of you. You may not be able to change the world, but you can change your world. And that kind of change has the power to impact generations to come.

Defying Your Limitations

What is your dream? What do you desire? What is holding you back? What are you willing to sacrifice for what you truly want?

We only have one life. While we cannot change the past, the decisions we make in this moment will dramatically impact our future.

How long will you allow the nagging voices of insecurity to continue to overwhelm the restrained yearning and craving in your soul to make a difference? What will the decisions you are making today speak to future generations?

Whatever is holding you back from your best must stop immediately if you are going to progress from where you are now to where you need to be. Get up and take a walk to your nearest mirror. Face it and take a good long look. The person staring back at you holds the key to progress. You already have everything inside of you that you need.

If the culture that shaped you contradicts your dream destination, it has to be confronted and removed as an obstacle to your desired future. You are the one who holds the power to your greatness, not your naysayers and critics. If it's past mistakes that are holding you back, know that you can redeem the failures of yesterday by making better decisions today.

Take every negative thought into captivity, defy the odds, and realize that if you didn't have odds to face, you wouldn't have a real victory to celebrate. It's going to cost you, but it's worth the price. Nothing worth having ever comes cheap. It's time to get your fight and resolve back. No matter the obstacle or challenge you're facing, you have the power to overcome. Hear the voice of purpose and destiny calling you onward. Take authority over your life and circumstances.

Decide that, starting today, you will defy every limitation that has held you back from the life you were created to live.

This is your moment.

ACKNOWLEDGMENTS

The experience of writing a book is profoundly unique. It is much more difficult than I thought it would be but more rewarding than I could have ever imagined. I could never attempt to write and publish a book in which I know will help so many without acknowledging and thanking those who are responsible for who I am today. The Creator of life and the universe is who I am most thankful for. God is my source of life, my Father, and his Son, Jesus, is my Savior. I have a relationship with him. If not for that relationship I would be a train wreck. He is my everything.

Then, there is my wife. There is not a more angelic soul on this planet. Next to Jesus Christ, she is my heartbeat, my joy, inspiration, and reason to wake up every morning. This book would not have been possible without her because the life I live today would not have been possible without her. Thank you, Tommie, for relentlessly and authentically loving me, supporting me, and most importantly, for sticking with me through every season and transition for all these years. And for giving me two amazing gifts—my two incredible sons.

Tim and Caleb, you'll never know this side of heaven how profoundly proud I am of the men you have both become. It is an honor to be your father. Thank you both for making this book a reality. You are the context of the message on its pages. Claire and Sofia, in my heart I have adopted you as daughters. Not only are you both an answer to prayer, but you also complete my sons. Parents only dream their sons will marry the caliber of women you are. I love you both with all my heart and am thankful for your impact in the lives of my sons, as well as mine. You've both taught me so much and are major contributors to the significance of this book's message.

Now, what grandfather would write a book without mentioning the little souls who bring unspeakable joy to living—my grandchildren, of course. My oldest, Violet, has unknowingly provided so many powerful points and nuggets in this book. It is she who so vividly demonstrates the beauty of a free-spirited, risk-taking, creative, and visionary approach to life. I will never forget the power of those tiny fingers as they bend back and forth on an extended arm and as she resolutely looks at me and says, "C'mon, Pop!" This has remained a consistent reminding inspiration whenever fatigue, doubt, and second guessing have had the tendency to creep into my faith. I can hear her now: "Let's go! We have places to go and things to do–C'mon, Pop!" Violet is my princess. Fitz is my pal. He is light-hearted and chill. Easy like Sunday morning. Never in a rush or hurried. He embraces every moment with reluctant curiosity. Noah is our newest. He is my pal as well. His gaze is captivating. He's strong like his father and will no doubt be as competitive.

Outside of my family, there are so many I owe my deepest gratitude for believing in me when I didn't believe in myself. It has been the authentic relationships in my life that have made the deepest and lasting impact. The number of them are too many to mention. If you're reading this, you know who you are. You unselfishly invested value and wisdom into helping me become a better version of myself. I humbly thank you.

ABOUT THE AUTHOR

Tim Gautreax believes that the key to a fulfilled life begins with a healthy mindset.

For more than 30 years, Tim has trained individuals and teams in the realm of human behavior and personal development. His deep understanding of how people think, feel, and behave gives him the constructive insights he needs into what may be preventing an individual from reaching their full potential.

Tim has proven experience and results in organizations consisting of up to 5,000 people in multiple locations. This has also given him an impressive edge in effectively building and leading large staffs.

Tim is a specialist in organizational culture and health. In addition, he has mentored CEOs and presidents of corporations where it relates directly to individual and organizational health and development.

Tim has had plenty of exciting opportunities to instruct leadership training programs throughout United States and around the world. Whether it's for a start-up business or a large corporation, Tim's message always rings clear: "To get what you've never had, you'll have to do what you've never done."

Tim and his wife, Tommie, have been married for 37 years and have two sons and daughters-in-law and three grandchildren.

Defy Your Limitations is his first book.